"*The Great Chasm* has dres̲ ̲ ̲ ̲ ̲ ̲ ̲ ̲ ̲ ̲ in 21st century clothing. In c̲ ̲ ̲ ̲ ̲ ̲ ̲ something of our own poverty. After years of sojourning with those on the margins, Derek Engdahl has earned the right to do some exegesis from the edges. He tells stories from his experiences in a way that bring Luke's manuscript into focus. We are given lucid prose to see afresh how it relates to our world today. *The Great Chasm* is a work which will help close today's chasm between rich and poor."

—**Scott Bessenecker,** Associate Director of Missions for InterVarsity Christian Fellowship and author of *The New Friars: The Emerging Movement Serving the World's Poor*

"As idealistic justice-makers, we encounter complex bridge-crossing experiences as we enter into the midst of global poverty. Derek has anchored reflections on these issues in a solid Biblical exegesis, providing a platform for genuine economic divide-crossing spiritualities. He does us this service from his years of leadership of engagement with the issues globally with Servant Partners, built on an Intervarsity background of digging deep in the Word of God.

—**Viv Grigg,** International Director, MA in Transformational Urban Leadership, Azusa Pacific Seminary and author of *Cry of the Urban Poor*

"Great books aren't merely written by authors but written into the hearts and souls of the people authoring them. Derek Engdahl is a great author and *The Great Chasm* is a great book—not only because of what Derek illuminates about the Gospel of Luke, but how these truths are embodied and reflected in the way Derek lives, loves, and services the world. You can trust that as you flip through these pages, a holy imagination emerges from the credibility of a life well-lived.

–**CHRISTOPHER L. HEUERTZ**, CO-FOUNDER OF GRAVITY, A CENTER FOR CONTEMPLATIVE ACTIVISM AND AUTHOR OF *UNEXPECTED GIFTS: DISCOVERING THE WAY OF COMMUNITY.*

"This book isn't for everyone—only people who own some money. Although you don't need much of it to profit from Engdahl's wisdom. Engdahl's stories and insights into Scripture challenged me, motivated me, and encouraged me. An investment in *The Great Chasm* will yield rich benefits."

–**DAVID T. LAMB**, ASSOCIATE PROFESSOR OF OLD TESTAMENT, BIBLICAL THEOLOGICAL SEMINARY AND AUTHOR OF *GOD BEHAVING BADLY: IS THE GOD OF THE OLD TESTAMENT ANGRY, SEXIST AND RACIST?*

"Derek Engdahl challenges our lives of comfort by drawing on the scriptures that likewise challenge our comfortable lifestyles. Integrating many compelling stories, he calls us to take wealth and poverty seriously, just as the Bible does. If you desire to see the gospel lived out and the chasm between rich and poor bridged, read this book."

–**JUDE TIERSMA WATSON**, ASSOCIATE PROFESSOR OF URBAN MISSION IN FULLER SEMINARY'S SCHOOL OF INTERCULTURAL STUDIES. SHE LIVES IN A STRUGGLING IMMIGRANT NEIGHBORHOOD IN LOS ANGELES AS A MEMBER OF INNERCHANGE/CRM.

THE GREAT CHASM

THE GREAT CHASM

HOW TO STOP OUR WEALTH FROM SEPARATING US FROM THE POOR AND GOD

Derek W. Engdahl

SERVANT PARTNERS

Servant Partners Press
P.O. Box 3144
Pomona, CA 91769

www.servantpartners.org

Servant Partners is an interdenominational evangelical missions
agency that sends, trains, and equips those who follow Jesus
by living among the world's urban poor. By the power of the
Holy Spirit, we seek the transformation of communities with the
urban poor through church planting, community organizing, and
leadership development.

Cover design: Loren Roberts
Cover art: Derek W. Engdahl

Published in association with Samizdat Creative, a division of
Samizdat Publishing Group (samizdatcreative.com)

The interviews for this book were conducted by the author
between 2008 and 2013 and are used by permission.

print ISBN: 978-1-938633-25-6

CONTENTS

For my wife, Lisa

INTRODUCTION

IN 1998, I SPENT A COUPLE OF DAYS WITH RAY AND ANNIE IN their squatter home in a Manila slum. Conceptually, I knew there was real poverty in the world—I had even seen some of it—but I had never *lived* in it, not like this. I had never personally known people who endured such destitute conditions until that moment. For a few days, they opened their home and their lives to me. They lived in a very small house with a dirt floor. The living room/dining room/kitchen area was about eight by ten feet. Huge rats ran through the house and under the sink while we ate together. They feared neither us nor the slum cats, which were not large enough to threaten them. The bathroom was a corner of the room separated by a shower curtain. The house had no running water, so in order to bathe you had to fill up a large barrel and then pour water over yourself with a small bucket. The sewage from the toilet ran straight out to the canal behind the house. Even though the canal was only a couple of feet deep, you could not see the bottom through the blackened water.

A rickety ladder led to the loft that served as the bedroom for the family of five. Three children slept on a full size mattress, and the married couple slept on the floor in a corner of the loft separated by a curtain. While I was with them, Ray and Annie gave me their mat and slept with the children. I stared up at the ceiling as I fell asleep that first night. It was very hot and humid. Street noise loudly filled the room. The ceiling was made out of found objects, the most prominent of which was a sign advertising fish for sale. As I struggled to sleep with the heat and the fear of visits from corpulent rats and two-inch flying cockroaches, I thought, no one should have to live like this.

I was newly engaged at the time and carried some pictures of my fiancé to show to people. Ray took one of the pictures—of the rose I had given her when I proposed—and meticulously lacquered and framed it for me with the tools he had. I was moved by how much effort he put into making it beautiful, and he was visibly proud of it when he presented it back to me. It was the first of many gifts from the poor to be displayed prominently throughout our house.

I had never thought of myself as a rich person. I was raised in a middle-class family and have lived much of my adult life in the lower portion of that category. But in Manila I realized I was, in fact, very well off. Ray and Annie's life is not that unusual. Half of everyone on earth now lives in an urban center. Of that half, almost one in every three people live in a slum. While the percentage of slum-dwellers relative to the larger population has been falling over the last twenty years, the overall number continues to climb.[1] As a whole, about fifty percent of the world lives on less than two dollars a day.[2] I easily could have been born into poverty without much chance to alter my circumstances. As an asthmatic, I might not have had access to medicine and hospitals like I did here. I might not have survived childhood. I might never have gone to college, gotten a job, owned a car, or bought a house— things that most middle-class Americans take for granted. I took my wealth for granted, giving little thought to those who had so much less. Though I knew people like Ray and Annie existed, I did not personally know them or their struggles. It was easy to ignore the plight of the faceless poor, but it was harder to ignore them once I saw them as real people—as friends.

There is a great divide between the rich and poor of this world. Half of the world's population lives on less money per day than many of us spend on one coffee from Starbucks. Some people live in mansions, while others take shelter in cardboard boxes. Some pay to lose weight, while others starve to death. Some are planning for their retirements, while others struggle to make it through the day. Both groups may have knowledge that the other exists, but they can hardly relate to each other's experience.

We are all aware that we do not all live at the same level, but a problem arises when we try to identify who is rich and who is poor. Can only those who are at the extreme ends be called "rich" and "poor," or is there some dividing line that puts us all in one category or the other? It might depend on one's perspective. Those of us living as middle-class Americans rarely think of ourselves as rich, yet we are to people living in American ghettos and barrios, not to mention people in majority world slums.

The poor are equally difficult to define. Those who fall

under the poverty level in Western society often live with greater material comfort than those at the bottom of society in poorer countries. Are they then not truly poor? Poverty and wealth are, in some ways, relative, and yet we know them when see them. People with resources naturally insulate themselves from those they consider poor. My wife and I bought a house in a gang-ridden, inner city neighborhood in 2002. When we were looking for a house, we gave our realtor the instructions that we were not interested in living in a neighborhood that was too nice. She replied that in her forty-some years in real estate, she had never heard that request. That is because people usually seek to live in the best—i.e. wealthiest, safest, best educationally equipped community they can afford. They move away from areas that they may consider dangerous or less than what they and their children deserve. This is, after all, the American dream; we naturally seek what we consider to be better lives for our families. To do otherwise is even considered irresponsible by some.

Our lifestyles and where we choose to live are normally dictated by income and education. We tend to surround ourselves with people who are like us. It's simply more comfortable. This impulse also affects what churches we attend. It has been said that eleven o'clock in the morning on Sunday is the most racially segregated hour during the week, but I would guess that the class divide in our country is at least as great as the racial one. Very few congregations are socio-economically diverse. Even churches that boast of their cultural diversity often draw people from the same socio-economic class. Ultimately, we want our church experience to be comfortable, to meet our needs as we see them. If we are educated, we gravitate to congregations that have other educated people. If we are affluent, we seek out congregations with people of similar lifestyles.

Most of us do not have deep relationships with people outside our social class. And sadly, the church has almost nothing to say about this. On any given Sunday, thousands of sermons are preached, but how many Christians are hearing about God's concern for the poor, his demands for justice, the dangers of wealth, or the need to lay down one's life in service to our poor brothers and sisters in Christ? I am not convinced that the whole gospel is being proclaimed weekly.

We are still faced with questions about who the poor are, however. Which level of poverty deserves our generosity? Are there righteous poor and unrighteous poor, those who are worth helping and those who are not? Can we assign a dollar amount that divides who will be considered poor and who will be rich? Who exactly is my poor neighbor?

An expert in Jewish law asked Jesus a similar question in Luke 10. Jesus responded with a parable about a Samaritan who, unlike some Jewish religious leaders of the time, had compassion on a victim of robbery and beating. This parable is usually interpreted as a story of how a disliked, second-class citizen—the Samaritan—overcame prejudice to love a man who would be his enemy. But as a friend once pointed out to me, the text is unclear about the victim's identity. We do not know if he is Jewish or not, wealthy or poor, a good person or an evil one. He was stripped naked, leaving nothing to identify him. He never speaks. Perhaps he was unconscious the entire time. All we know is that he was in need, and maybe that is all the Samaritan knew as well. Jesus does not mention anything about the victim's identity because it does not matter. The point is that the Samaritan did not care about any of those things; to him, the victim was a neighbor who needed to be helped.

In the same way, the poor are those who are powerless or vulnerable. They are victims of injustice and lack the resources to meet their needs or easily change their lives. If we were in their situation we would want to be helped. We don't have to determine exactly who is truly poor, or righteously poor. We only have to love our neighbors as we love ourselves.

Some of my friends have argued that we should not use the term "poor" at all since it carries such negative connotations. Many who suffer from poverty might be uncomfortable describing themselves as poor and could perceive our use of the language as another form of oppression. This is a valid point. Yet there is a biblical distinction between those who are comfortable and those who are in need. If we lose the language for that, we could end up losing the underlying issue. I think it is particularly important for those of us who are "rich" to understand that there are people in situations different from ours. We also need to be sensitive to the fact that those we would consider "poor" may not feel similarly about themselves, nor might they refer to their communities as "slums," though someone from an affluent perspective might label them as such.

I remember as a child visiting a friend of my mother who lived in a poorer part of town. We were dropping her child off when my friend who was with us said, "They live *here*?" I unfortunately replied, "Yeah, the slums." My mother overheard me and took me to task for being incredibly elitist and insensitive (though she did not use those exact terms). Obviously that was hurtful to our poorer friends. It implied that I thought I was better, that I looked down on them. I do not believe we can really wrestle with the topics of wealth and poverty without using such terms as "rich" and "poor"—but I hope I do so with sensitivity.

I also need to clarify that when I use the terms "rich" and "poor" in this book, I mean the materially rich and poor. This is an important distinction. As we will see, those who are materially poor can be rich in other, more important ways, while the materially rich often suffer from other forms of poverty. It is also important to note that the term "poor" is sometimes used positively in Scripture, just as the term "rich" is sometimes used negatively. We don't need to shy away from these words; we simply need to recapture their full meanings.

Even when there are great differences in actual material wealth, there are often similar patterns within poverty situations. Many of the same issues are found in poor communities around the world, despite the variances in material wealth within those communities. People in the inner cities of America feel the same powerlessness as those in the slums of Asia. The same vices surface in Los Angeles as they do in Bangkok: alcoholism, drug addiction, gambling, participation in the occult, and violence. These are things people often turn to when they are despondent and frustrated, desiring to escape their lives. Poverty is not simply a lack of money. While it is related to money, it is fundamentally a result of dysfunctional relationships.

In his book *Walking with the Poor*, Bryant Myers explains this idea well:

The poor are poor largely because they live in networks of relationships that do not work for their well-being. Their relationships with others are often oppressive and disempowering as a result of the non-poor playing god in the lives of the poor. Their relationship within themselves is diminished and debilitated as a result of the grind of poverty and the feeling of permanent powerlessness. Their relationship with those they call "other" is experienced as exclusion. Their relationship with their environment is increasingly less productive because poverty leaves no room for caring for the environment. Their relationship with the God who created them and sustains their life is distorted by an inadequate knowledge of who God is and what God wishes for all humankind. Poverty is the whole family of our relationships that are not all they can be.[3]

This dysfunction exists even in the most affluent nations.

If we really knew our poor neighbors, we would understand that their struggles are greater than merely a lack of income. However, since most of us move away from poor neighborhoods if we have the means to do so, we quickly become detached from our neighbors' needs.

One of the first books I remember reading on the topic of wealth and poverty was *The Call to Conversion* by Jim Wallis, the founder of Sojourners. In it he wrote that the rich might have concern for the poor, but rarely have true compassion. Concern is feeling bad when you see something bad happen to someone else. Compassion, on the other hand, is seeing your brother's pain and believing that you cannot let him continue to suffer in that way. Compassion requires real relationship: "That is precisely what the affluent lack with respect to the poor—any real feeling of relationship. We have no relationship with the poor because we have no proximity to the poor."[4] Jim Wallis first challenged the church about this issue over thirty years ago, and even though many have responded, his description of American society, and the American church, is still largely true.

In 1998, I joined Servant Partners, an organization that ministers to the urban poor around the world. As a white, middle-class man, I moved into a working poor neighborhood in the city of Pomona on the eastern edge of Los Angeles County. I began a journey of downward mobility that has brought me into deeper relationship with people very different from myself. Others have been doing the same thing for decades, people who have been influenced by the teachings of John Perkins, Viv Grigg, Ray Bakke, Robert Lupton, Robert Linthicum, Tony Campolo, Jim Wallis, and others. Their prophetic voices have called thousands of people to live among the poor and have inspired a new generation of prophets as well. While these voices were important in my decision to relocate to a depressed Latino community, it was Scripture that convicted me that loving the poor and working for justice were not optional as a Christian, but rather fundamental to what it means to be a disciple. I have come to believe that how we relate to the poor of this world affects our salvation because it affects our relationship with God. One cannot know Christ and not know the poor; to ignore the needy, the oppressed, and the helpless is to ignore Christ himself.

This truth is evident in Scripture. Poverty and wealth, the rich and the poor, are major themes throughout the Bible. Jim Wallis said, "Jesus talked more about wealth and poverty than almost any other subject, including heaven and hell, sexual morality, the Law, or violence."[5] Though it may not get much attention on Sunday morning, this subject is very important to God, and this book is an effort to prove that case. I wish I could provide a very thorough look at every passage that deals with the poor and the rich in the Bible, but as such a pervasive subject, it would require more space than I have. Instead, I want to focus mainly on the 16th chapter of Luke. The majority of the chapter is taken up by two parables: one about a shrewd manager and the other about a rich man and a poor man named Lazarus. Reflecting deeply on these two parables, as well as looking at other related Scriptures, we will begin to gain a fairly thorough, but by no means comprehensive, portrait of God's feelings about the poor and the rich—and how we as followers of Jesus are supposed to respond.

In the second parable in Luke 16, a rich man ignores the plight of a poor man, Lazarus, outside the rich man's gate. When they die, angels carry the poor man to Abraham's side, while the rich man goes to Hades. God in his justice reverses their roles—the rich man now experiences agony, and Lazarus, comfort. A great chasm is fixed between them, a gorge so massive that no creature could cross from one side to the other. For once you are on one side, you are there for eternity. Before they died, the rich man and the poor man were also separated by a chasm—a socio-economic divide. Their lives were radically different, and they had no connection to each other. The rich man never saw Lazarus as his neighbor and, therefore, never sought to leave his comfortable life to care for him, even though he passed Lazarus every day. He did not show mercy to others in his earthly life, so in the next life he was shown none.

A number of years ago, I was again in Manila, this time visiting a poor village on the outskirts of the city. To get to the village, we had to cross a rope bridge that was suspended over a gorge. The villagers used this bridge every day to connect to the larger world. Having little fear of heights, I led the way for our group, jumping out onto the wooden boards. About ten feet out, the boards began to crack under my weight. The bridge was used to carrying svelte Filipinos, not well fed, two-hundred-pound

Americans. I instantly slowed my pace, respecting the danger of the task I was undertaking.

Crossing a chasm is never easy. It is costly, awkward, and scary, and we will likely make many missteps. But while the great, eternal chasm cannot be crossed, the chasms in this life—the ones that separate us from each other, the rich from the poor—can be. The question is: will we get on the bridge while there still is one?

1

LOVING THE LOST

Now all the tax collectors and sinners were coming near to listen to him. And the Pharisees and the scribes were grumbling and saying, "This fellow welcomes sinners and eats with them."

So he told them this parable: "Which one of you, having a hundred sheep and losing one of them, does not leave the ninety-nine in the wilderness and go after the one that is lost until he finds it? When he has found it, he lays it on his shoulders and rejoices. And when he comes home, he calls together his friends and neighbors, saying to them, 'Rejoice with me, for I have found my sheep that was lost.' Just so, I tell you, there will be more joy in heaven over one sinner who repents than over ninety-nine righteous persons who need no repentance.

"Or what woman having ten silver coins, if she loses one of them, does not light a lamp, sweep the house,

and search carefully until she finds it? When she has found it, she calls together her friends and neighbors, saying, 'Rejoice with me, for I have found the coin that I had lost.' Just so, I tell you, there is joy in the presence of the angels of God over one sinner who repents."

Then Jesus said, "There was a man who had two sons. The younger of them said to his father, 'Father, give me the share of the property that will belong to me.' So he divided his property between them.

"A few days later the younger son gathered all he had and traveled to a distant country, and there he squandered his property in dissolute living. When he had spent everything, a severe famine took place throughout that country, and he began to be in need. So he went and hired himself out to one of the citizens of that country, who sent him to his fields to feed the pigs. He would gladly have filled himself with the pods that the pigs were eating; and no one gave him anything.

"But when he came to himself he said, 'How many of my father's hired hands have bread enough and to spare, but here I am dying of hunger! I will get up and go to my father, and I will say to him, "Father, I have sinned against heaven and before you; I am no longer worthy to be called your son; treat me like one of your hired hands."' So he set off and went to his father.

"But while he was still far off, his father saw him and

was filled with compassion; he ran and put his arms around him and kissed him.

"Then the son said to him, 'Father, I have sinned against heaven and before you; I am no longer worthy to be called your son.'

"But the father said to his slaves, 'Quickly, bring out a robe—the best one—and put it on him; put a ring on his finger and sandals on his feet. And get the fatted calf and kill it, and let us eat and celebrate; for this son of mine was dead and is alive again; he was lost and is found!' And they began to celebrate.

"Now his elder son was in the field; and when he came and approached the house, he heard music and dancing. He called one of the slaves and asked what was going on. He replied, 'Your brother has come, and your father has killed the fatted calf, because he has got him back safe and sound.'

"Then he became angry and refused to go in. His father came out and began to plead with him. But he answered his father, 'Listen! For all these years I have been working like a slave for you, and I have never disobeyed your command; yet you have never given me even a young goat so that I might celebrate with my friends. But when this son of yours came back, who has devoured your property with prostitutes, you killed the fatted calf for him!'

"Then the father said to him, 'Son, you are always with me, and all that is mine is yours. But we had to

*celebrate and rejoice, because this brother of yours
was dead and has come to life; he was lost and has
been found.'"*

—*Luke 15:1-32, NRSV*

ANUMBER OF YEARS AGO, I WAS ON MY WAY TO VISIT OUR
Servant Partners team in Bangkok, Thailand. There was
a bit of a crisis, and it was important that I get there as soon
as possible. I got in line at the airline counter and pulled out
the folder where I keep my passport. As I was doing so, I
realized that in my haste I had not double-checked to see
if my passport was still in the folder before I left the house.
As I opened the folder my fear was confirmed; my passport
was gone. Slightly panicked, I got out of line and called my
wife to see if she could find it. It was after eleven o'clock at
night and our daughter was asleep, but I hoped that if my
wife could find it, someone could make the hour drive to
the airport and get it to me. I had just enough time to make
the flight if someone left in the next few minutes. After looking for quite some time, she called me back to tell me that it
was nowhere to be found. I had evidently lost it after coming through customs on my previous trip. It was gone for
good. I started to feel sick. I felt irresponsible for losing my
passport. I felt anxious about having to contact the team
and tell them I was not going to be there the next day, maybe not for another month. There was nothing I could do
but return home and start the process of obtaining a new
passport. It was amazing that the loss of so small a thing
could affect my life so much.

If you have ever lost anything valuable, you know the overwhelming panic, fear, and sadness it can cause. That feeling is exponentially greater when the thing that is lost is a person. Every parent has probably experienced a moment when they thought their child was gone; even if it only lasts for a couple of seconds, it is the worst feeling in the world.

Luke 16 opens with Jesus teaching his disciples. The scene, however, really begins in Luke 15 with an interaction between Jesus and the scribes and Pharisees.[1] The more I have studied these chapters the more I believe they should be looked at together. Understanding the parables of the lost sheep, the lost coin, and the lost son will help our understanding of the context of chapter 16.

Years ago, I attended a leadership conference at Willow Creek Church in Illinois. Bill Hybels spoke about an epiphany he had one day while reading the 15th chapter of Luke. He realized that by repeating the images of the lost three times, Jesus was emphasizing just how important the lost are to him and, therefore, how important evangelism is. Though I agree with Hybels' observation that Jesus is very concerned for the lost, I do not think this passage is primarily about evangelism, at least not in the sense that we often think of evangelism.

The section begins with a complaint from the Pharisees: Jesus is eating with tax collectors and sinners, something no truly religious person should be doing. Despite the fact that he seems to be a righteous person, he actually welcomes and socializes with the dregs of society.

He responds to the religious leaders' indignation with these three parables, all of which have some basic similarities as well as differences. Rather than attempting to interpret each parable to its fullest, I will focus on just a few relevant elements.

All three parables are about something lost. In context, it is clear that the lost things represent the tax collectors and sinners. Each lost thing—from each parable—belonged to someone at one point; the sheep belonged to the shepherd, the coin belonged to the woman, and the son belonged to the father. Each lost thing was also part of a larger whole; the sheep was part of the flock, the coin was one among many coins, and the son was part of a family. In turn, each becomes lost, separated from the larger whole; the sheep wanders off from the flock, the coin is separated from the rest of the coins, and the younger son decides to leave his family. The tax collectors and sinners who Jesus ate with were at one point part of the Jewish family of God, but they had wandered off—from both God and his people.

In each of the parables, there is also an extensive search for that which has been lost. The shepherd leaves the ninety-nine to look for the one that wandered off, the woman lights a lamp and searches her whole house for the coin, and the father, though he gives his son the freedom to leave, keeps watch for him on the road, which is why he is able to see him at a distance. This was Jesus' ministry. He was finding the lost and bringing them back home. This is different from what we traditionally consider evangelism. The general mission of evangelical Christians is to reach people for the first time, people who have never known God, who do not believe in God. These tax collectors and sinners, on the other hand, were at one point in relationship with God. They were the children of Abraham, people of the covenant. Their problem was not that they did not believe in God, but that they had become "sinners" because of the lives they had chosen, or that had been thrust upon them. And in becoming sinners, they were estranged from the rest of the family as well as from God.

We often read these parables through strictly spiritual lenses. The lost, we might say, are lost spiritually because they have wandered from God and chosen lives of sin. But in the context of these parables, we realize that their "lost-ness" is also social, economic, and even political. Joachim Jeremias defines "sinner" as:

> (1) people who led an immoral life (e.g. adulterers, swindlers: Luke 18:11), and (2) people who followed a dishonorable occupation (i.e. one that notoriously involved dishonesty or immorality), and who were on that account deprived of civil rights, such as holding office or bearing witness in legal proceedings—e.g. customs officers, tax collectors, shepherds, donkey drivers, peddlers, and tanners.[2]

I wonder if the poor and disabled might have sometimes fallen into the category of sinner as well, since their misfortune might have been thought of as the result of unrighteousness. Even the disciples seemed to hold this worldview (John 9:2). The lost, then, were those who were cut off not only from God but also from the rest of their family, the rest of the sheep, the rest of the coins. They were out-casts, condemned by the larger social order. They suffered both from the consequences of their actions and from the judgment of others. The fact that the Pharisees would not consider eating with such people only emphasizes the fact that their estrangement from the religious establishment was not completely their own choice.

The last parable makes this point most clearly. When the younger son decides to ask for his inheritance and leave the father, he loses everything. When studying this pas-sage, I questioned why Jesus goes into so much detail about what happens to the son after he leaves. If the par-able were just about spiritual "lostness," the point could have been made fairly succinctly. He could have squan-dered his money and ended up impoverished. That would have been enough to suggest that his choice was fool-ish and that life with the father would have been better. Instead, Jesus spends a good deal of time on the many hardships that befall the younger son. I believe that these details are important in order to understand in what ways people become, or are, lost.

The younger son certainly initiated his own hardship. He demanded his inheritance early so that he could be-come independent and live the life he desired. He broke relationship with his father and the rest of his family and left for a foreign land, not realizing how much his father, and his own home, had to offer him. He ran off to some first century version of Las Vegas to indulge every carnal desire. Eventually his money ran out and his life in the fast lane came to an abrupt end. In a brief moment, he spent a lifetime of wealth. So when a famine came he had no resources to fall back on. The famine was not a consequence of his sin, but his sin made him vulnerable.

When he had to get a job, he ended up with the worst job a good Jewish boy could have—feeding pigs. This would have been revolting to him, probably equivalent to an American feeding sewer rats. More importantly, the scholar I. Howard Marshall argues that the ancient Jews would have considered feeding pigs an unclean occupation. Helping to raise pigs would have been strictly forbidden for an obedient Jew.[3] In order to survive, the son chose a job that was not only shameful but that he knew was sinful. He was so destitute he longed to eat the pods he was feeding to the pigs. In other words, the pigs were better taken care of than he was. His employer exploited his vulnerability, not even paying him a livable wage. No one gave him anything; he received no mercy from anyone. The nation of Israel was commanded to care for the sojourner and the poor, but in that foreign land the younger son had no such safety net. He was truly lost.

Through this parable, Jesus summarizes the various states of those around him who had become lost and impoverished. Some people had chosen to gratify their selfish desires and had lost their relationships with God as well as their fellow Jews. Others were victims of circumstances beyond their control—famine, drought, or disability—and perhaps others were victimized by oppression. For some, the choice may have initiated a downfall. For others, their misfortune or mistreatment may have led them to turn to what was considered sinful activity. In any case, these lost and impoverished people had no one who showed them mercy.

I once visited Aling Nena at her home in Manila. Viv Grigg had written about her in his book *Companion to the Poor*—she was his landlord is a slum called Tatalon. Though I knew her story through Viv, this was the first time I had gotten to hear it from her. She told us how her husband died unexpectedly, leaving her without any income. In order to afford food, she would hold up taxi drivers at knifepoint. It was hard to imagine this tiny woman being able to rob grown men of their fares. She opened a gambling den and rented out rooms in her home for additional income. In order to ease her suffering, Aling Nena turned to drink and became an alcoholic. Eventually, she came to Jesus and turned her life around, becoming a pillar in the local church. Her story is not only an example of how a person can become lost, but also how disasters strike and force decisions that send life into a tailspin. The "sinners" who sought out Jesus—and who the Pharisees looked down upon—were lost not only spiritually, but also socially and, in many cases, economically. Grigg has observed that the causes of poverty seen in the Bible can be put into three categories: personal sin, calamity, and oppression by others.[4] The younger son falls into all three.

Eventually the younger son realized that life with his father would be far greater than what he was enduring. He knew that his father's hired hands were treated justly.

Because of his sin and the insult against his father, the son did not believe he had any right to be taken back as a son, but if he could become a servant, at least he would no longer be suffering in poverty. This situation begs the question as to whether he truly repents for his actions or whether he simply does the math and realizes that he would be better off returning home. I would argue his repentance in this moment is essentially genuine. Understanding that he would be better off with his father and turning from the disappointing life he had voluntarily chosen exemplifies the essence of genuine repentance. Helmut Thielicke wrote of this parable:

> When the son thinks he has come to the end of his road, then God really begins his way. This end, from man's point of view, and this beginning, from God's point of view—this is repentance. . . . It was not because the far country made him sick that he turned back home. It was rather that the consciousness of home disgusted him with the far country, actually made him realize what estrangement and lostness is.[5]

The people who suffered from their own choices, as well as from things done to them, were the ones that flocked to Jesus. When they encountered Jesus, they realized he offered them something invaluable that they had lost—a way back to the Father and out of the deprivation they had experienced.

One of our Servant Partners staff members was raised in a squatter community in Manila. She ended up marrying an American who had voluntarily moved into her community to serve the poor while he was in graduate school. After their schooling—she was in college at that time—they were married and continued to live in the same squatter community. The first time they went back to his home in the United States, she told her husband that she wished he had never brought her to America. All she had ever known was the slum; now she knew how middle-class Americans lived. The experience of American wealth exposed the poverty she lived in. Before that poverty was just reality; now it was a choice. They did follow God's call to return to the slums, but her eyes were forever opened to the suffering there. Encountering Jesus opened the eyes of the lost. In him they saw wealth that exposed the poverty they had become resigned to. In him they found the acceptance and mercy that they had been cut off from.

The father longed for the younger son's return. When he saw him in the distance he had compassion on him; he sprinted out to him and embraced him. Compassion was his first response just as it was for the Good Samaritan. Luke tells us that they both "see" and then "have compassion." The father did not dwell on how his son had sinned against him and the family. He had not rehearsed an "I told you so" speech. His emotion was not anger, self-satisfaction, or disgust. It was compassion. Between these two parables—the Good Samaritan and the lost son—Jesus gives us examples of his own motivation, which we are to emulate. When we see those in need, our response should be compassion—because it is Jesus' response. It is the divine response to suffering.

Many things can block our sense of compassion. The Samaritan could have been more concerned about his time and money than the man who was beaten by the robbers. If he had known the victim to be Jewish, he might have been glad that tragedy had fallen on an enemy. He could have thought that this man was someone else's responsibility. Similarly, the father could have been bitter toward the prodigal son. He could have believed that his son had gotten what he deserved for his poor choices. Any of these thoughts can keep us from feeling sympathy towards those in need, but they are all related in one way: they are all symptoms of selfishness. If we are consumed with self-protection, self-justification, and self-gratification, then compassion is impossible.

The father's compassion led him to respond in a remarkable way. He did not listen to the son's well-rehearsed speech meant to get him back into the house as an employee. Instead, he welcomed him back as a son, restored all of the family honors upon him, and celebrated with a feast. He cared little about the disrespect shown to him, as his only concern was the safe return of his son whom he loved.

Rejoicing over what has been found is another element that is common to all three parables. We are naturally happy when finding something that was lost, especially if that object has great value. When we lose something, we often think we have lost it forever; we mourn its loss. So if we find it again, it is like new life. When the son leaves, the father considers him not only lost, but also dead. His return, then, is as if he has come back to life. Surely that is cause for joy.

Those of us with children know that it is difficult to explain the love we have for them. It is hard to put into words. You do not choose to love your children; you love them because they are part of you. When young, they are dependent upon you, and you are the world to them. We love our children even when they do things that make it hard for us to love them, and sometimes this means making agonizing decisions. I have a friend whose son struggled with drug addiction. He was making life for the whole family unbearable. They tried many things to help him but nothing worked. One day, my friend and his wife changed the locks on their house when their son was out. When he returned, they told him he had to find somewhere else to live until he got his life in order. Eventually, he did deal with his life and was welcomed back into the family. Their love for him never ceased—even when it meant sending him away.

Jesus offers us an intimate glimpse of himself and his Father with this last parable. He considers sinners and outcasts his children. He loves them like his own because they are his own. Even though they have made bad choices or are considered the least in society, they are no less important or valuable than those who stayed home like "good" children. In these three parables, Jesus emphasizes the importance of the whole, united community. He is not content with the ninety-nine sheep or the nine coins or the one older son; he wants the whole. Which is why the lost are of special importance; if one is gone, something is always missing. We all understand this unique value for the lost. If you had several children and one was tragically kidnapped, you would not think, "Oh well, we have three other kids. We won't miss little Suzy." Rather, you would make every effort to find the one who had been separated from you. Instantly, everything else would become less important. As parents, we understand that no matter how many children we have, we could not bear to lose one. The same is true with God and his children.

The father in the parable is overjoyed by the restoration of his family; the older brother, however, is not at all happy with the younger son's return. Paralleling the Pharisees' contempt toward Jesus when he welcomed tax collectors and sinners, the older son does not respond with compassion. In the older son's mind, the younger son did not deserve to be taken back into the family. He had sinned. He had disgraced his respectable family while the older brother continued to labor tirelessly on behalf of the family. The older brother was outraged that such a son not only would be welcomed back, but celebrated as well. He refused to go to the party for his brother, choosing to stay outside.

When the father learned that his oldest son was outside, he left the party to beg him to join the celebration. The older brother responded, "Look, I have been slaving away for you for years and I never disobeyed you. And you never even gave me a cruddy little goat to have a party with my friends. But *this son of yours* comes back having used up your wealth on prostitutes and you throw him a huge party.

How is that fair?"

To which the father replied, "Son, you are always with me, and all that is mine is yours. It was right for us to celebrate, because *your brother* was dead, and is alive; he was lost and is found."

This story is fundamentally about relationships; the relationships between the father and his two sons, and the relationship between the two brothers. Neither son had a very good relationship with the father. The younger son believed that the world had more to offer than his old man, not realizing how good he had it until he had lost everything. Even then, he never imagined just how gracious and extravagant his father was. The older brother also had a distorted relationship with his father. He viewed himself as a servant in the household. He slaved away, believing that if he worked hard enough he would inherit the estate when the old man died. The father reminded him that everything he had was already his; he was not a servant but a son. But more importantly, the son was always with the father. The father does not condemn the older son, but rather honors him.[6] He affirms that it was good he stayed. However, the son was so focused on working away for a future reward that he neglected the present relationship with his father. The Pharisees were in the same boat. Jesus did not condemn their desire to be righteous, but they, too, misunderstood the Father. They considered him a boss, not a parent.

It is interesting that when the older son goes on his tirade, he refers to the younger son as "your son," but when the father responds to him, he calls him "your brother," a point I italicized above. The older son was happy to cut off his delinquent brother; the misfortune that his younger brother suffered likely reinforced his view of himself as the good, responsible son. While his father was looking to the horizon, hoping to catch a glimpse of his lost child, the older brother was busying himself in the field. Ultimately, what the father wanted was for the older son to be truly glad that his brother was back. After all, the injury was done to the father not the brother; it was the father's wealth that was squandered. If the father could forgive the younger son, why shouldn't the older brother?

The point of the parable is that the whole family should rejoice when the lost is found, just as the father does. The repentance of the son is somewhat secondary. Despite the fact that we call this the story of the Prodigal Son, he is not really the focus of the story: "In the end it is not so much the repentance of the son as the communal joy of the restored and reunited family which is the culminating note in the parable."[7] Jesus, like the father in the story, was appealing to the Pharisees to be joyful over the return of their lost siblings. Unfortunately, the Pharisees felt the same way as the older brother; namely, they were happy to cut off the unworthy. They did not see these sinners as brothers and sisters needing to be brought back into the family, but as unfaithful servants deserving to be condemned. Their sin made the Pharisees feel more self-righteous because they had avoided becoming like them.

I think we may view the poor in this same way today,

especially those who have chosen sinful lifestyles. Most of us are politically correct enough not to say things like, "The poor get what they deserve because they are lazy or stupid or sinful", but we subconsciously believe that we are not in their situation because we are a little better than they are. Examine your heart and see if I am right. The human heart loves to justify itself. We compare educations, incomes, positions, possessions, our accomplishments, and the accomplishments of our children—even our own holiness. Could it be that the poor make us feel better about ourselves?

The older son told the father that he never disobeyed his command, but when the father begged him to enter the party, he refused. He had not been obedient to his actual father, but to his own idea of who the father was. He had become estranged from the father because he would not love as the father loved.[8] The parable ends unresolved; we do not know if the older son goes in or not. It stands as an open invitation to the Pharisees; they can stand on the outside, angry that Jesus would welcome such undeserving people, or they can join the celebration and be glad that their brothers and sisters have returned to the family. Jesus wanted them to join the party; he wanted them to be restored to their outcast siblings. But to do so, they would have to change their view of God and their relationship with him.

The Father wants the family reunited. The goal is not only to bring people back to God, but also to bring them back into the social and economic networks that can sustain their physical lives. Maybe this is evangelism after all. It is not just about getting people to say a certain prayer and join a church, but to restore relationships. The poor of this world are often cut off; they are not treated as part of the larger family of humanity. This is true even in the Church. The average local suburban congregation may have sympathy for those suffering in poverty, they may even have some programs that help the poor, but they still do not treat the needy as lost family members who need to be brought back into relationship. They do not see them as siblings for whom they are morally responsible. We treat them as "God's Children," not "Our Brothers and Sisters."

It is tempting to draw a line separating those we feel responsibility for and those we do not, those who are like us and those who are not. That inner circle may be as small as our individual persons or our immediate families, or as broad as our class, cultural group, or nationality. At some point, most of us make a distinction between "us" and "them." However, we have no place creating such divisions. Jesus has already instructed us in Luke that the greatest commandments are to love the Lord our God and to love our neighbors as ourselves. The two are related. To be in a healthy relationship with the Father means loving the younger brother, precisely because the Father loves him. It is to see him as a brother, precisely because the Father considers him a child. In the parable of the Good Samaritan, Jesus redefines what it means to be a neighbor. The Samaritan was a good neighbor because he cared for the needy person despite potential cultural or socio-economic barriers. In the parable of the lost son,

Jesus redefines the idea of neighbor itself. The outcast is not merely a neighbor, but a sister or a brother.

While the Japanese evangelist Toyohiko Kagawa was a student, he was diagnosed with tuberculosis. The man who led him to Christ, Dr. H. W. Myers, paid for his hospital stay, but not wanting to burden his mentor, Kagawa moved into a fisherman's cottage in Tokyo where he preached the gospel to local fishermen. Because of his disease, no one wanted to get close to him. He was lonely. Myers came to visit him and stayed with him in the cottage, even sharing his bed. Kagawa asked why he was not afraid of him.

"Your disease is contagious," Myers said, "but love is more contagious."

Kagawa later wrote:

At that moment, I realized more truly than ever what love really means: that love can have no fear; that love can have no limits; that love encompasses everything—the people sick like me and the people sick in spirit and mind. I thought I must love everybody too—even the horrible people in the slums. I decided I must not be sick anymore. I told God that if He would let me live I would serve His children in the slums. Pretty soon I began to get well again.[9]

The Father has that kind of limitless, fearless, contagious love for us. Despite our sick and miserable conditions, he embraces us, seeing us only as the children he cares so much for. This unconditional love—incarnated by Dr. Myers—taught Kagawa to love without restrictions. Kagawa moved into the worst slum in Japan and continued to proclaim the gospel. He took in the homeless, diseased, and mentally ill. He was robbed, threatened, and beaten, but he remained in the slums.[10] Over his lifetime, Kagawa led thousands to Christ and worked tirelessly on behalf of the poor by improving the quality of life in the slums, establishing orphanages, setting up credit unions, and organizing labor.

The Father's love should transform us. The fact that God loves us despite our ugliness should change us into people who love even those who seem ugly to us or to society as a whole. The Pharisees were unable to care about their outcast brothers and sisters because their relationship with their Father was not based upon love; it was about work, righteousness, and rules. It is difficult to give love if we are unfamiliar with receiving it. If we have a hard time caring about the lost in this world, then we need to begin with our relationship with our Father. I often think about Paul's words in Galatians 2:20: "I have been crucified with Christ; it is no longer I who live but Christ who lives in me; and the life I now live in the flesh I live by faith in the Son of God, who loved me and gave himself for me." Paul—a Pharisee himself at one point—underwent a great transformation of faith because of his experience of Jesus' love and sacrifice for him. His Savior's love was not abstract, theoretical, or theological; it was experiential.

Experiencing God's sacrificial love enables us to love sacrificially. Loving our brothers and sisters means seeking them when they are lost. It means having compassion on them, welcoming them, and rejoicing over them. It means being reconciled to them as they are reconciled to the Father and restoring them to their rightful place in the family, treating them as brothers and sisters and not as projects. Simply put, it means loving them as God loves them. The lost are not just those who do not believe in God; they are those who have become estranged from him and the rest of their family. Therefore, being "found" is more than coming into a saving relationship with God; it is the restoration of all relationships, based upon a true relationship with the Father. Understanding this truth will help us understand Jesus' teachings about our relationship with and responsibility to the poor.

2

A DISHONEST MANAGER'S EXAMPLE

Then Jesus said to the disciples, "There was a rich man who had a manager, and charges were brought to him that this man was squandering his property. So he summoned him and said to him, 'What is this that I hear about you? Give me an accounting of your management, because you cannot be my manager any longer.' Then the manager said to himself, 'What will I do, now that my master is taking the position away from me? I am not strong enough to dig, and I am ashamed to beg. I have decided what to do so that, when I am dismissed as manager, people may welcome me into their homes.' So, summoning his master's debtors one by one, he asked the first, 'How much do you owe my master?' He answered, 'A hundred jugs of olive oil.' He said to him, 'Take your bill, sit down quickly, and make it fifty.' Then he asked another, 'And how much do you owe?' He replied, 'A hundred containers of wheat.' He said to him, 'Take your bill and make it eighty.' And his master com-

*mended the dishonest manager because he had
acted shrewdly; for the children of this age are more
shrewd in dealing with their own generation than are
the children of light. And I tell you, make friends for
yourselves by means of dishonest wealth so that
when it is gone, they may welcome you into the eternal homes."*

—*Luke 16:1-9*

A WHILE AGO I WAS PART OF A MEETING BETWEEN OUR SMALL
inner city church and a large, local, affluent suburban
church. As leaders, we were talking about ways we could
partner together and bless each other. Though much
larger and better resourced than we, the leaders of the
suburban church were very humble and desired that our
relationship be truly reciprocal. As we shared ideas of how
we could help each other, one of our church members,
Tom Hsieh, volunteered an idea. He shared that, at one
point, he and his wife were making about $200,000 a year
but felt called by God to live on $40,000 and give the rest
away. They did this year in and year out. At that point, Tom
quite sincerely offered himself as a resource to help others learn to live more simply and give away most of their
money.

There was a moment of deep, awkward silence. I could
almost hear the air molecules buzzing past my ears. I
laughed a little bit and moved the discussion on. These
were godly people, but it was clear from their silence that

they were not interested in learning to live on a fraction of what they had become accustomed to. Nor did they seem convicted that simplicity and generosity were issues they needed to wrestle with as part of their own discipleship.

How can we blame them? The church, as a whole, does not teach consistently on wealth, and churches that do often misuse Scripture. Money is a sensitive topic in most congregations. If you are a pastor, you do not want to offend the wealthy people in your church. They might feel judged and, potentially, take their gifts elsewhere.

I understand the tension. As missionaries, my wife and I have raised our own support for over twenty years, and some of our largest supporters are pretty well off. Of course, we would not want to lose their support, but more importantly, we would never want them to feel that we are passing judgment on them. While it is easy to avoid discussing money and lifestyle issues, money was a common topic in Jesus' teaching, and as with all of Jesus' difficult teachings, we have to look at them for what they say, not what we wish they said. The parable of the shrewd manager is one of those very challenging teachings. But it is meant as an encouragement to pursue life—both in this age and the one to come.

From verse 1 we know that the intended audience for this parable is Jesus' disciples, but from verse 14 we learn that there is a larger group listening in. As we discovered in the previous chapter, this section is a continuation of the scene that begins in chapter 15 and includes the Pharisees, scribes, tax collectors, and sinners as well. This parable, therefore, has significance for both the disciples and the larger group, but the former are the primary audience.[1] There is no question that this is one of Jesus' trickiest parables. It is hard to use a negative figure to illustrate a positive example, but that is, in fact, what Jesus does here.

In the parable, a rich man received a report that his manager had been wasting his possessions. The word "wasting" here is the same word used to describe the younger son's activity in the previous chapter, so we know that the accusation was more than mismanagement; it was severe negligence. Presumably, this steward was in charge of managing his employer's accounts, keeping record of his assets and the debts people owed to him. Jesus does not inform us if the accusation against the manager is correct or not, but the employer believed the report and told his manager to settle the books and get out. Some large businesses escort employees out of the building immediately after they are terminated for fear that, in their wrath, they will sabotage the company with whatever tools are left at their disposal. Such suspicion would have served the rich man in the parable well; instead, he left his manager alone to deal creatively with his newfound unemployment.

The manager began to consider his situation. Who would hire him to be a manager if he failed to do his job well? He was not strong enough for manual labor. He was too proud to beg on the streets. In short, he was out of options and facing a future of poverty and death. Then he came upon a brilliant idea: using the resources still under his control, he would lessen the amounts owed by his master's debtors. They would be so grateful, he believed, that they would take him into their own homes and care for him when he is kicked out. In forgiving some of their debts he extended them a form of grace, trusting that such mercy had the power to return the blessing.

He asked each debtor what was owed his master, which, one would think, he should know as his manager. Perhaps this is evidence that the master's assumption about his incompetence was correct, or maybe he did know what they owed and he wanted each person to verbalize their debt to emphasize what he was doing for them.[2] In any case, each one owed his master significant sums, probably more than they could easily repay. The fact that the manager told them to "sit down quickly and write" a lesser amount seems to imply that he was inviting them to participate in his plan to defraud his master. It is possible the manager was simply aware that word would soon get out about his ouster and that he needed to act swiftly before it was discovered he had no authority to alter the debts.[3] But by being asked to act quickly themselves, the debtors would have to realize they were accomplices in some nefarious act. Despite the subterfuge, the debtors gladly took advantage of the steward's current situation for their own benefit. Though they might not have been obligated to take him in, you have to figure that they would have been pretty grateful and therefore fairly likely to help him out.[4]

Verse 8 seems like an unexpected twist. The rich man somehow found out what had happened and actually commended the manger because he acted shrewdly. We would expect him to have been upset with his former employee, and perhaps even himself for his own oversight. Instead, he had some admiration for the manager's cleverness, enough to praise him for it. He realized that his manager was able to use resources that did not belong to him to buy a future for himself. It is not that the rich man thought what the manager did was good; he thought it was smart.

Jesus highlights the point he wants us to understand: "For the children of this age are more shrewd in dealing with their own generation than are the children of light." It is not the dishonesty, but the example of shrewdness that Jesus wants "the children of the light"—his disciples who are seeking to lay up treasure in heaven (Luke 12:32-34)—to get from this story.

The unexpected response of the rich man and Jesus' use of the manager as a positive example have led scholars to wonder if what the manager had done was, in fact, dishonest. Some have speculated that the manager was actually acting like some kind of first century Robin Hood by redistributing wealth to the poor that the rich man had gained either through oppressive means or by usury.[5] Others have argued that the manager was merely subtracting the interest that he had tacked on himself, a common practice of the day, and was, therefore, giving up his own profits.[6]

But the text and more recent scholarship do not support these interpretations. Though the rich are never described positively in Luke, Jesus does not tell us just how this rich man acquired his riches, nor does he describe any oppression or usury. If he wanted us to believe that the manager was acting righteously, he would have included that information. Any interest that the manager was collecting himself would not have been on the official books of debts owed to his master and so the reduction could not have come out of his own pocket.[7] The evidence also seems to suggest that the debtors were not poor; they had amassed more debt than a poor person would seem capable of, they were educated enough to be able to write, and they had sufficient resources to take in the manager if they wanted to.[8] There is nothing in the text that suggests the manager had acted justly. Rather, Jesus describes the manager as dishonest in verse 8 and includes all of the actors, including the debtors, as examples of "children of this age," as contrasted with "children of the light." The manager had mishandled funds and taken advantage of his boss, the debtors were not bothered by his dishonesty as long as it benefited them, and the rich man, however he came by his wealth, cared less about honesty than fiscal creativity. They were all unscrupulous people.[9] Trying to justify the manager's actions as righteous misses the point of Jesus' teaching.

The tension created by the rich man's praise, and by implication, Jesus' praise, is resolved if we make a distinction between the manager's dishonest activities and his cleverness: "The steward is praised for his shrewdness in decisively providing for the future at a critical moment, not for the fraudulent or dishonest means he utilizes to do so."[10] Jesus expects us to be disturbed by the unrighteous way the "children of this age" use money to manipulate the world for their own benefit. But he wants us to learn a lesson from them about how our resources can produce good things for us if we are smart.

Jesus wants us to focus on what it means to be shrewd with our wealth. It is important to note here that Jesus does not merely mean our money. The word translated here as "wealth" in the NRSV is, in the original text, a transliteration of the Aramaic word *Mammon*, which can mean money but also suggests the larger idea of wealth in general, anything we use to provide for ourselves.[11] Wealth is an even broader concept now than it would have been in first century Palestine. In our current world, we have salaries, benefits, bonuses, investments, retirement accounts, properties, collectables, insurance, credit, and all those possessions that we believe we need to survive and thrive. All these things contribute to our wealth.

In this passage, Jesus teaches us that we have to use our wealth intelligently and that, in this area, we can learn a great deal from worldly people. Specifically, they understand how it can be used to ingratiate others. The people of God, on the other hand, underestimate the real power of wealth.

In our city, we battled against the construction of a waste transfer station in a poor part of town. It would have been the thirty-second site dedicated to the processing of some form of trash in our city. As proposed, this new facility would be a regional center, drawing from the eleven cities around us and adding another six hundred diesel truck trips through an already polluted community every day.

And yet there was a great deal of support among city leaders for this project. One of the main, though unstated, reasons people were supportive was that the proposed area for the site was poor. In the past, more affluent neighborhoods had successfully blocked this project. The second reason for the widespread support was that the company proposing the project had been spreading money around the city for the past ten years just for this moment. They had given money to local politicians and non-profits, including the Boys and Girls Club, of which one of the owners of the company was board chair. They threw parties and invited all the influential people in the city. They sponsored citywide events like the mayor's State of the City speech. They approached a council member who opposed the project and offered to renovate one of the parks in her district if she changed her position. And most insidiously, they created and staffed an organization called the Coalition for Environmental Justice to protest the expansion of a competitor's project that was identical to their own.

They had spent millions of dollars winning friends and indebting people to them. While it is possible that they genuinely wanted to do some good, it was also quite evident that there were strings attached. One thing is very clear: like the manager in the parable, they knew what money could buy and were very shrewd with their wealth.

Sadly, much of the world works this way. It did in Jesus' time, and it does today. So just what is Jesus getting at in this parable? Are we supposed to use our wealth like the world does? In verse 9, Jesus gives us the insight we are to draw from this parable: we are to use dishonest (some translations say "unrighteous") wealth to gain friends so that when it is gone they will welcome us into eternal homes. By "dishonest," Jesus does not mean wealth that is gained dishonestly; rather there is something inherently dishonest or unrighteous about *Mammon*. I will discuss the spiritual power of *Mammon* in a later chapter as Jesus continues his teaching on wealth. Here, the quality that stands out is that—like the manager and his master—*Mammon* is tied to this present world. It ultimately fails us.

I am reminded of a story a friend told me about his grandmother in South Carolina. She was pestered by an ambitious and greedy neighbor who wanted to buy some of her land, which she did not want to sell. "I don't know why he needs all that money," she said to my friend in her sweet southern drawl. "He can't take it with him." She paused thoughtfully before continuing, "And if he could it would all just burn up anyway."

We can't take our wealth with us (wherever that final destination may be). Like the manager who was being fired, we only have temporary usage of our material resources. We, too, are only stewards of another's wealth. The temptation is to believe that it will not fail us, that it will always be there to protect us if we are careful with it. But our earthly wealth is not permanent; it always fails, so we must use it while we have it. We are supposed to use it to make friends who will be able to welcome us into eternal homes.

It is much easier to be generous toward our friends once we realize that our wealth is not ours to keep. If we use it only for our own earthly benefit, we underestimate its real potential. The children of the light must think in terms of the eternal benefits that wealth can bring, not merely of its earthly comforts.

Jacques Ellul cautions that there is a danger in this idea of stewardship. The danger is that we might come to believe that, as stewards, we are somehow worthier of trust than others and therefore have some authority over the recipients of our largesse. We may believe that since God has entrusted us with wealth, he has also entrusted us with directing the affairs of the world.[12] The idea behind this is that by giving money away we are "buying" some kind of product and should therefore have influence over that product. The rich and generous do sometimes think this way, but this idea is not in agreement with biblical stewardship. Jesus' point is not that stewardship gives us some special right or authority, but rather a special responsibility to use our resources according to God's will. In the context of Luke 16, that responsibility is to use it to benefit our friends.

Who are these "friends" that Jesus is talking about? Like in the parable, they are those who are in debt and need relief. Within the larger context of Luke, it is evident that Jesus is referring to the poor, since concern for the disadvantaged is such a large theme in the gospel. In the third chapter of Luke, when asked what they needed to do in order to "bear fruits worthy of repentance," John the Baptist told the people that if they have two coats, they should share with the person who has none; and if they have more food than they need, they should give to the person who has less. Concern for the poor and hungry is an act of repentance. When John sent two disciples to Jesus to see if he was in fact the Messiah (Luke 7:18-23), Jesus tells them to inform John about what they had seen and heard—the blind receive their sight, the lame walk, the lepers are cleansed, the deaf hear, the dead are raised up, and the poor have good news preached to them. Jesus' ministry to the poor and broken was a sign that he was the chosen one from God. In chapter 12, he told his disciples to sell all they had and give it to the poor. In chapter 14, Jesus taught people not to invite their friends or relatives when they throw a feast, but rather to invite the poor, crippled, lame, and blind. Being generous to those who could not repay in kind would guarantee repayment at the resurrection of the righteous. In the parable of the Great Banquet, the poor, crippled, lame, and blind are the ones who end up at the feast of the kingdom of God after those first invited turn down the Great Master.

Our earthly wealth, rather than being stored up or lavished upon ourselves, should be used to bless others, particularly the needy, and they, in turn, will receive us into eternity. Jesus does not mean to imply that they somehow offer us salvation. He does not claim that they welcome us into *their* eternal homes, which would parallel the parable, but into *the* eternal home that, implicitly, God has created for us all. Nor does this mean the poor get a free ticket into the kingdom by virtue of their poverty. In the parable of the Great Banquet, the poor, needy, and social outcasts enter the kingdom because they recognize its great worth. Those who were first invited end up skipping out on the party because they had other concerns they believed, or at least claimed, were more important—land, oxen, and wives. The poor and disabled had no such distractions. Their poverty did not get them into the banquet, but it helped them value it more. Those who flocked to Jesus evidence this; many were the least in society. To them, Jesus offered a new hope, a new wholeness, a new wealth that they had never known. It was the rich and powerful who had a hard time dealing with Jesus. If this seems less true in today's society, it is most likely because we have overlooked some of Jesus' teachings. His point in the parable of the Great Banquet is that we are going to be surprised by who ends up in the kingdom. The poor, oppressed, and social outcasts will likely greatly outnumber those who had lives of privilege or apparent righteousness.

The theme of receiving people into one's home is also significant in Luke. In Luke 9:5, Jesus tells his twelve disciples to shake the dust off their feet of those towns that do not receive them. In Luke 9:48, he teaches them that whoever receives a child in his name receives him and the one who sent him. When the seventy are sent out in Luke 10:8-9, they, like the twelve earlier, are told to stay in the house of those that receive them until they leave that town. Mary and Martha receive Jesus into their house in Luke

10:38. And in Luke 15:2, Jesus was accused of receiving tax collectors and sinners and eating with them. From these passages we see that the idea of receiving means to accept, bring in, care for, and serve. The parable of the Great Banquet implies that those who are poor now will not always be so. In the eternal kingdom they will be in imperishable homes, allowing them to welcome and bless those who were generous to them in the previous life.

Just because wealth is temporary does not mean that it is useless to the people of God. People need a certain amount of resources to survive—Jesus acknowledges that our Father knows we do (Matt 6:32)—but many of us have more than we really need. If we have extra wealth, we should use it to assist those suffering in poverty. In return, those godly poor who are blessed by us will joyously welcome us when we join them in the eternal kingdom. Homeless people for whom we not only bought food but listened to and treated as human beings, children from tough backgrounds whom we welcomed into our homes, single mothers whom we loaned money to so they could get through hard times—Jesus seems to say that they will be in a place to accept us, love us, and welcome us.

There may be occasions where giving money to people directly does not actually help them. It might be better to offer to buy a homeless person food rather than hand him or her some change that could be used to fuel an addiction. Even better would be taking the time to listen to that person and see if there are ways to help get him or her off the street. Personally, I feel that it is important to be generous even if I know I am being lied to or that the person might not use it well. They have to answer to God for their choices, and I don't need to control them.

One Christmas Eve we were driving to my mother-in-law's house, and at the end of the exit ramp stood a homeless man begging for money. Since it was Christmas Eve, I decided to be especially generous and give him two whole dollars. I handed him two bills as the light was changing and wished God's blessing upon him. A couple of minutes later, it dawned on me that I had a hundred dollar bill in my wallet, which was a Christmas gift from a friend. At the next light, I check to see if I had inadvertently given the homeless man that bill. I had, in fact, done just that. My immediate response was dread, but I quickly realized that perhaps God wanted me to be more generous than I had been willing to be on my own. When I gave the change out of my pocket it never really cost me anything. I never had to give anything up. But this gift was costly. I prayed that the man felt God's generosity to him since I knew it was not my own generosity that led to the gift.

I imagine Jesus could have encouraged his followers to give generously to the temple so that it could care for the poor in a more systematic way. However, he puts the responsibility upon the individual to meet the needs of other individuals with whom they are in relationship. As we look at other passages we will see that this is a pattern that runs throughout Scripture, starting in the Hebrew Bible. God is more concerned with the poor than with poverty. The needy are not an abstract concept for him that must be dealt with on a macro level; to him, poverty is primarily an issue of personal suffering. Jesus commands us to love the poor, not to end poverty. That is not to say that he is not concerned with the larger issues of systemic injustice, oppression, and deprivation, but that is not where we should begin. We begin with a relationship. As my friend John Hayes wrote, "Poverty, we know about. It's poor people we do not know; but it's *knowing* poor people that enables substantive change and authentic empowerment to take place."[13]

When my wife turned fifty we threw a big party for her, but instead of requesting gifts she asked that people give us cash that we would send to our friends in Mexico who were struggling to put their kids through college. Growing up in poverty, our friends had few options but to work in low-paying jobs, but they knew if their children received college educations the next generation would be more stable financially. When we lived in Mexico they were the first people to welcome us into their home despite their poverty. We spoke little Spanish and could barely communicate with them, but they put up with us. They helped us figure out how to navigate daily life in their city. They treated us like family.

In Leviticus 25, God instituted the Jubilee, where every fifty years everyone who had lost land had it returned to them. It was a corporate redistribution of wealth. We thought that since it was Lisa's Jubilee birthday, it was appropriate to redistribute a tiny bit of our wealth to those who needed it more. A few weeks later, we were able to present the money to our friends in Mexico in person. It was enough to allow their son to finish his schooling. They knew it was an answer to prayer. Giving them a wad of cash was not strange because they have become family and we knew what would help them. It is common for family members to help each other out. Jesus is simply challenging us to rethink who we consider family. He intends that we view our poorer friends as part of our family, people with whom we have a reciprocal relationship, just like the father in the earlier parable encouraged his older son to view his younger brother.

When I first moved to the inner city, I lived in a dilapidated and mismanaged apartment complex. Because it was pretty inexpensive, most of the residents living there were recent immigrants or families struggling to survive. We met the Ramirez family very early on. Rachael had four children from a couple of different men, one of whom was in prison. Her five-year-old son, Jonny, became a fixture in our apartment. Every evening he would come up to say goodnight before he went to bed. He was also fascinated with our mouthwash and would routinely ask to "wash his mouth" before leaving. His father was not reliable, and I think that my roommate and I became sort of surrogate fathers for him. Because Rachael had no transportation, I would drive her to her errands. When the county took custody of her oldest child, she would borrow my truck to visit him. (She jokingly began to refer to it as "her" truck.) When her oldest daughter began to fall behind in school and her teacher recommended that she buy a Hooked on Phonics set to bring her back up to grade level, some of the other

Servant Partners people living in the complex bought it for her. Within a couple of months, her reading caught up with the rest of the class.

Being invested in the Ramirez family was chaotic at times. Rachael's life, as is true for many poor people around the world, was just one crisis after another. Some were brought on by herself and her own poor choices, others were the product of her limited resources and the systems that took advantage of her. As an example, when I was moving out of that apartment complex, I asked the manager to do a walkthrough with me to determine what I needed to do to get my security deposit back. She informed me that I did not need to do any cleaning or repairs since nobody ever got their deposits back. I informed her that that was illegal and asked for the number of the management company. I called every day for a week, but only ever got an answering machine. When I finally reached someone, they told me that my deposit had been used already to replace the carpeting that they claimed I had destroyed. I requested that they send me an itemized list of what they used my deposit for, which they were legally obligated to do. Nothing ever came. I realized that if I, a college educated person with some understanding of the law, was having trouble getting what was legally mine, how much more difficult must it be for my neighbors with limited knowledge of their rights or poor English language skills.

Eventually, Rachael moved back east to be with her mother, and I lost contact with them. The last I heard, they were doing well. The kids were excelling in school and she was working. Before she left, she gave me a small gift she had made herself as an expression of her gratefulness. We may never see them again in this lifetime, but I imagine that if they continue to follow Jesus, we will see them in the kingdom. And then any sacrifices that people made for them will seem small.

Future blessing from those we bless in this lifetime is only part of the benefit suggested by the parable of the Dishonest Manager. The manager in the parable sought to insure some future security for himself. In the same manner, our generosity toward those in need must come out of our hope for salvation. The poor are not able to offer us salvation, but how we treat them and how we use our money is related to our salvation. We most certainly are not justified by how we spend our money—no manner of self-sacrifice or benevolence can merit salvation—but the manner in which we use our wealth does reveal something about our relationship with God.

As John Piper puts it, "Generosity confirms that our hope is in God and not in ourselves or our money. We don't earn eternal life. It is a gift of grace (2 Timothy 1:9). We receive it by resting in God's promise. Then how we use our money confirms or denies the reality of that rest."[14] Robert Linthicum puts it a little more bluntly: "Eternal life is not received simply by faith. It is received by a faith that is demonstrated through a redistribution of our money . . . for the purpose of eliminating poverty."[15] In other words, our faith and our trust in God must look like something. Just as John the Baptist insisted that true repentance must bear "fruit" and not merely conviction of sin, our faith cannot exist by mere words or beliefs; there must be actions.

Stinginess toward our poor brother or sister indicates that something is wrong in our relationship with God. The Apostle John makes that point emphatically: "How does God's love abide in anyone who has the world's goods and sees a brother or sister in need and yet refuses to help?" (1 John 3:17) A lack of generosity also demonstrates a warped relationship with wealth—where it can become the source of our hope instead of God. As we will see over the next few chapters, our concern for our needy brother and sister, and our generosity toward them, is an indicator of just how healthy our relationship with God truly is.

Let's not get ahead of ourselves. This parable is not really about the consequences of being greedy, but the blessings for being generous. Jesus assumes that if we are following him we will want what is good and holy and true. He wants us to enter into life. He wants us to store up treasure, but the kind of treasure that is eternal, not temporary. He does not think that our desire for security is wrong; it is just that we often invest in things that cannot give us the kind of security we really need. Our goal should be to make friends and seek homes that last for eternity. We need to use our borrowed resources shrewdly to "buy" that which cannot perish.

3

THE FAITHFUL USE OF WEALTH

Whoever is faithful in a very little is faithful also in much; and whoever is dishonest in a very little is dishonest also in much. If then you have not been faithful with the dishonest wealth, who will entrust to you the true riches? And if you have not been faithful with what belongs to another, who will give you what is your own?

—Luke 16:10-12

JESUS CONTINUES HIS TEACHING TO HIS DISCIPLES WITH A COUple of truisms. If you are faithful with a little, you will be faithful with a lot. If you are dishonest with a little you, will be dishonest with a lot. We all instinctively understand this. It's why parents talk about getting their children a goldfish before they can have a dog. They want to see that their children are responsible with small tasks before they take on large ones. (Based on my own daughter's care for her goldfish, no dog would survive a week in our house.) The same is usually true in the work world. You have to prove yourself reliable in small situations before you can be trusted with larger responsibilities.

When I was a teenager, I worked for K-Mart. I started at the lowest position in the store—Vista 7, they called it then. It meant that I did whatever task the assistant managers determined needed to be done in the store, from stocking shelves to cleaning up spilled Icees and other more questionable liquids, to bailing cardboard boxes (which was kind of the highlight of the job). Basically, I did everything that no one else really wanted to do—and everyone was my boss. Eventually, I was promoted to a department. I left for college but returned to K-Mart every summer. I kept moving to different departments, but I never had to be a Vista 7 again, even though I was gone for most of the year. I had proven myself worthy of much greater responsibilities—mixing paint, watering plants, driving the forklift, even occasionally running a cash register, which I never did very well.

I had to prove that I was responsible before they gave me the keys to the forklift. One of the Vista 7s I started with eventually became an assistant manager. How reliable we are with small things is a test of whether or not we are ready for larger responsibilities. The converse is also true. If someone is dishonest with something small, it is probably a sign that they will be dishonest with larger responsibilities. It would be foolish to entrust the company's payroll to someone who, as a cashier, stole money from the cash register.

Given that how we deal with small things is an indicator of how we deal with large things, Jesus asks two rhetorical questions. The first is, if you have not been faithful with dishonest wealth, who would entrust you with true riches? Wealth, perhaps surprisingly, is the "very little" thing that we are given. Good incomes, nice homes, luxury cars, dining at great restaurants—these are the perks of success in our society, the rewards for hard work. Advertisers often remind us that we deserve such rewards and that they mark an exceptional life. But in the kingdom of God, earthly wealth is a very little thing—the goldfish, the Vista 7 job. It is our faithfulness in the small things that determines whether we can be entrusted with more.

The second rhetorical question Jesus poses is, if you have not been faithful with that which is someone else's, who would give you what is your own? Worldly wealth, as we talked about in the previous chapter, is not really ours. We are only stewards of it for a limited time. Whenever we borrow something from a friend or neighbor, we should feel a special responsibility for that possession. It should be taken care of, and if something happens to it, we should offer to fix or replace it because we understand that it is not ours to use however we please.

In the same way, we should have an extra sense of responsibility for those things that God has entrusted to us. We should use them in accordance with how God would use them. In doing so we prove ourselves faithful and therefore worthy of being given that which is our own.

How, then, are we to be faithful with this little, borrowed

resource? Should we be responsible in a worldly sense? Protecting, insuring, investing, and of course, tithing a small part of it? From the parable we explored in the last chapter, it would seem that faithfulness with wealth looks like giving it away. This seems somewhat counterintuitive. As I mentioned above, if we borrow something from a friend, we feel an extra responsibility to take care of that item. We would not naturally believe we had the right to give it away to someone else.

But when it comes to the *Mammon* God has given us, faithfulness is measured not by how much we protect and build, but by how much we give away to those in need. God tests our reliability not by how "responsible" we are with our money, but with how reckless, how generous we are with it. The picture we get of God from the parable in Luke 15 is that he is recklessly generous. He does not protect his resources; he is extravagant. He lavishes his love and his wealth on the undeserving. He associates himself with the poor and marginalized. He sent his Son to die upon a cross in order to reconcile a rebellious world to himself. By worldly standards, he could be called irresponsible. But he is not of the world.

Jesus tells a parable in Matthew 18 of a man who owed a debt to his master so large he could never repay it through a lifetime of work. He deserved to be sold into slavery with his whole family to recoup some of the massive debt, but the master had mercy on him and forgave what he owed. As soon as he was forgiven, he went out and found a fellow servant who owed him a relatively small amount of money. Instead of having mercy on him when he could not repay immediately, the first servant had him thrown in jail. When the master found out what happened, he returned judgment for judgment and threw the servant in jail as well.

The parable is meant to illustrate Jesus' repeated teachings that we need to forgive each other, and that if we fail to do so, God will not forgive the much greater debt we have with him. We are recipients of his mercy. We must allow that mercy to have such a transforming effect upon us that it causes us to be merciful to others. If it doesn't, then we make light of the mercy we have received from God. You may know this from experience; if you have committed a great sin, repented, and received God's forgiveness, you know it is easier to forgive others. Once we truly understand how far we have fallen, what pain we have caused, how unworthy of God's love we are, and yet that he loves and forgives us despite our brokenness, we cannot remain unchanged. We cannot go away from a true experience of his mercy with no mercy to extend to our neighbors, whose debts to us are much smaller.

Extending mercy to others is the faithful use of the mercy God gives to us. In the same way, generosity toward others is the faithful response to the generosity he extends to us. God the Father, Jesus, and the Holy Spirit are the embodiment of generosity. It should not surprise us then that the faithfulness God calls us to mirror his own generous nature. In giving away our grace and our wealth to the needy around us we become more like him. Our wealth is given to us largely in order to be given away.[1] We are faithful with *Mammon* when we spend it freely on others.

That is not to say that we should never use our money for anything but the poor. There are five other categories of faithful usage that I see in Scripture.

Providing for Our Basic Needs

God desires that our basic needs be met. We are instructed to pray for our daily bread, which assumes that he is willing and able to provide it (Matt 6:11). There is nothing wrong in spending money to provide for our families or ourselves. We should never feel guilty that we have food and shelter—that is God's will for everyone. When I first started spending time in truly poor communities around the world, I did feel some pangs of guilt that I lived in a simple but comfortable home and never had to go without food. But I came to realize that those things were not luxuries. They are things that everyone is entitled to. Everyone in the world should have enough food, enough clothing, comfortable shelter, adequate work, and the ability to have hope for the future. But many people in the world do not have even these things, and the lifestyle of many others goes way beyond those basic needs. The list of what we "need" continues to expand. We *need* air conditioning. We *need* a second car. We *need* to send our kids to private schools, and they *need* to be involved with activities multiple days of the week. We *need* to have a 50" television and a satellite dish. I don't mean to imply that these things are absolutely faithless uses of money, but we do need to reconsider what we actually *need*. Paul reminded Timothy that if we have food and clothing, we should be content (1 Tim 6:8).

Providing for the Local Body of Christ

In Galatians 6:10, Paul writes, "So then, whenever we have an opportunity, let us work for the good of all, and especially for those of the family of faith." We are supposed to have a special concern for the local body of Christ. As soon as the church was blessed by the outpouring of the Holy Spirit at Pentecost it began to hold everything in common. The people of the church understood they had a responsibility to each other. In the same way, we have a responsibility to care for and be generous with those brothers and sisters in our fellowship. Our own little church in Pomona is a good example of what the Body should look like in this area. We certainly have our share of problems and are far from perfect, but the generosity of the members toward one another is often remarkable. People who have lost their jobs are assisted by others in the congregation. Those whose legal status has made it impossible to work have been "employed" by church members or simply given food or money to survive. People loan each other cars and share children's clothes and toys. We ourselves have often been the recipients of others' generosity when we have hit unexpected expenses.

The Body of Christ is not limited to one local entity either. When my wife ended her fifteen-year ministry with InterVarsity Christian Fellowship, staff workers, former students, and friends gave us ten thousand dollars for a down payment on a house. We were stunned. We had believed that home ownership would never be an option for us with our limited incomes in the expensive L.A. housing market, but the larger Body took our need as their own.

Paul also instructs the churches, based on the teaching of Jesus, to provide for those who make their living by proclaiming the gospel (1 Cor 8:14, Gal 6:6). Though he forfeited that right himself, he believes that the local church needs to support those leaders who take on the full-time responsibility of caring for the body. I think that his teaching on this sets a solid precedent for supporting our local churches. They have expenses that should be the responsibility of a local body.

Providing for the Mission of the Church

Paul's convictions were different when it came to the larger mission of the church. J. M. Everts notes that Paul seemingly never took money from a church he was ministering to at the time. "But after he established a church, he expected them to contribute to the cause of the gospel."[2] The churches in Macedonia and Philippi are mentioned as having sent gifts to him to help him in his work (2 Cor 11:9, Phil 4:10-20).

A few years ago my wife and I were visiting our friends Rev. Dr. Joseph and Florence Mante in Ghana, West Africa. Joseph is currently the president of a seminary there. One day we were talking about the history of Christianity in Ghana, and we started to discuss how missionaries often sacrificed their lives to bring the gospel to Africa. "You see how much they loved us?" Florence remarked. Western missions certainly have a mixed track record historically, but those lost lives did plant seeds that have grown into something remarkable. The African Church is vibrant.

There is still a great need for local churches and believers to support the expanding work of the larger church. There is still a need for Christian workers in the world. There are still people who have not heard the gospel or seen authentic, sacrificial Christian community. Christian workers need to be supported not only from the West, but also from Africa, Asia, and Latin America. One of our Servant Partners families is from Zimbabwe. Although that African nation has its own share of problems, Phillip and Beauty felt called to minister to the poor of Mexico. They have worked with us for several years, but have struggled to raise sufficient money to live on because of their own country's poverty. The American church should be excited to support such people who desire to join God's global mission to reach the lost. Certainly cross-cultural mission should not be limited to the rich. The expansion of the kingdom is undoubtedly a faithful use of our money.

Hospitality

The ministry of hospitality has long roots in Jewish society. In Genesis 18, Abraham compelled three travelers (who ended up being divine) to come into his tent so that he could have their feet washed, let them rest, and feed them. The sojourner in Israel was supposed to be protected and cared for (Exod 22:21, Lev 19:10, Deut 10:19). Hospitality was instrumental in Jesus' ministry as well as in the early church (Mark 9:29ff, Luke 7:36ff, 10:5-9, 10:38, Acts 10:6, 17:7). Paul commanded the church to "contribute to the needs of the saints (and) extend hospitality to strangers" (Rom 12:13). Hospitality was one of the qualifications for becoming a bishop in the church (1 Tim 3:2). Though he had no home to bring people into, Jesus himself modeled hospitality by washing the disciples' feet (John 13:5).

As Christians, we must open our homes to each other and to those who have no homes to go to. My mother-in-law is particularly strong in hospitality. She cooks meals all day for people in the neighborhood and for those who are too sick to do so for themselves. For Thanksgiving and Christmas, she has always invited anyone who did not have any other family to spend the holidays with. Our money, our possessions, and our homes should be used to bless those around us. Personally, I do not believe we should own anything that we are not willing to use for and on other people. If we are afraid of people using up, damaging, or stealing things we have, then maybe we should not have them. Our things are never worth more than any person, no matter how insignificant they are in the world's eyes. If there is any justification for possessing anything of value, it should be so that others can benefit from it as well.

Celebration

Celebration was also important in the life of Israel. They were commanded to come together three times a year just to celebrate what God had done for them. Jesus could have condemned such activity as wasteful, but he never did. He even gave instructions about how to behave at a dinner and whom to invite to a banquet (Luke 14:7-14). The father in the prodigal parable celebrated when his son returned. Jesus himself went to wedding parties and even brought the wine (John 2:9). Celebration should be a significant part of the Christian life. Richard Foster includes it among his famous list of spiritual disciplines.[3] God calls us to lives of joy.

Celebration does not necessarily require the spending of money, but it is fine to use money for this purpose. Money can make us anxious; we can become obsessed with how we spend it. When you have relationships with people who are poor, it is easy to feel that we should never spend any money that could be given to them instead. But when the disciples protested how wasteful it was for the woman with the alabaster jar of nard to pour it on Jesus' head, he rebuked them. They argued that it could have been sold and the money given to the poor. Jesus responded that the poor would always be with them and whenever they wanted they could do good for them. But he would not always be there (Mark 14:3-9). Her sacrifice was a celebration of Jesus' life, an appropriate use of resources to anoint his body for burial.

I believe it is good to be indulgent from time to time with

our resources in an effort to be thankful for what God has done and to be extravagant with one another. A number of years ago, one of our friends received a large bonus from his job. He decided that he wanted to use the money to take the whole team that was working in the city to Disneyland as a time of celebration. At the time, it cost well over $1,000 to take the twenty-five people on our team. It was an extravagant gift that we all still remember today.

All of these areas are legitimate and faithful uses of our resources. The problem is that using our wealth specifically for the poor often falls to the bottom of this priority list. Or we omit the poor from the other categories. We should be generous to the members of the body of Christ, but especially the poor members. We should support the mission of the larger church, but especially toward the unreached poor. We should practice hospitality, but especially toward the needy, the homeless, and the outcast. We should be free to celebrate, but we especially need to invite the poor into our celebrations, which was commanded in Israel's time (Deut 14:28-29) as well as Jesus' (Luke 14:13). We cannot take Jesus' encouragement to be faithful with unrighteous *Mammon* out of context. We are to be generous, particularly toward those in need.

Is it faithless then to invest money, to have a savings account, or to put money away for retirement? While there is no a simple answer for any of these questions, we can address them briefly in light of the principles we have already discussed. I think we certainly should seek to multiply our wealth if our primary intention is to have more resources to give away. John Wesley preached a sermon on this topic, entitled "The Use of Money," where he encouraged people to gain all they can, save all they can through living simply, and give away all they can. As long as they could do so without injuring others or themselves, he argued, people should feel free to maximize their wealth in order to be generous with it. Wesley practiced what he preached. He continued to live on about 30 pounds a year despite his rising income. At one point his annual income exceeded 1,400 pounds and he gave away 98% of it.[4] There are some people who, unlike myself, are gifted at making money. If people use this gift as a way to bless the poor, they can have a profound impact on the kingdom of God.

Saving money is a more complicated issue. In Luke 12:16-21, Jesus told a parable about a rich man who had an abundant crop one year so he tore down his storage buildings in order to build larger ones that could accommodate his new wealth. The man then assured himself that he would have an early retirement where he could eat, drink, and be merry for years to come. But as soon as he had done so, God required his life from him and he was never able to enjoy the future he had envisioned. God declared him a fool because all his hard work ended up benefitting someone else, which was not the rich man's intention. Jesus then drew this conclusion: "So it is with those who store up treasures for themselves but are not rich toward God" (Luke 12:21).

From this parable, it seems that one of the critiques Jesus has about storing up wealth is that we can deceive ourselves into thinking that our abundance will guarantee future security and ease when there is no such guarantee. Our lives might be cut short, and calamities and theft can destroy what we have invested. Additionally, when the rich man came into his good fortune, his immediate thought was about protecting it for himself and his future comfort, and not about his poor brothers and sisters who could be blessed by it. If his goal were to be rich toward God, he would have given some of his wealth away or considered how to use it for hospitality and not just for himself.[5] The point of the parable is that we should be making sure we are generous with our resources and not scheming for a future ease that may never come.

I do think that there is a place for modern financial planning if we do not lay up more than we need, and if our saving does not keep us from generosity. My wife and I have chosen to create some small investments to help us retire at some point. We realized that if we didn't do so our Christian community or our daughter would be forced to support us. We have been assured by our Christian brothers and sisters that we would be cared for if we ever came to a point of desperation, but we felt it was responsible to try to put some money aside so that their money could be freed up for needier people. As for our daughter, we would like her to have the freedom to do whatever God calls her to and do not want her to feel that her decisions are determined by how we have chosen to live our lives. We have also realized that investing gives us greater future resources to be generous with. We have never had much discretionary income, but if that were to ever change, we would like to turn that into greater giving and not simply greater savings. When, or if, we retire, we would like to be in a place where we could continue to give to others.

Some people might feel convicted not to save anything for the future because they believe it is important to be generous in the present and trust that God will provide for them in the future. If you have this conviction I would not wish to discourage you from trusting God. Many people who feel this way choose to be part of intentional communities that share their resources and look after each other. I am in full support of such fellowships, but they, too, are a form of financial planning. This model is less individualistic and may rely more upon God's miraculous provision, but in the end there can still be an assumption that people's investment in the community will provide for them in the future.

In 1 Timothy 5:4, Paul writes, "If a widow has children or grandchildren, they should first learn their religious duty to their own family and makes some repayment to their parents; for this is pleasing in God's sight." In verse 8 he adds, "And whoever does not provide for relatives, and especially for family members, has denied the faith and is worse than an unbeliever." The assumption in Paul and Jesus' time was that children and grandchildren would provide for elderly family members who could no longer work. This was their culture's retirement plan, as it is for many cultures around the world today. People simply did not plan for their future by saving so much as investing in the younger generation who would then take care of them later. It was a different kind of investment, but it was still a form of planning.

In Servant Partners, we allow people to put money into retirement accounts. Every time we orient our new staff, I tell them that they are not required to have an account (I do not even have one), yet I caution them that ten years down the road their convictions might change and they may wish they had put something aside when they were younger. I do not believe that Jesus is condemning people for planning for a future when they will no longer be able to draw an income. In fact, failure to consider our futures can result in becoming a burden to others without their consent. If we can save in such a way that is not excessive, and so that we continue to be generous now and into the future, then I think we are being faithful.

We have to remember that our material wealth is worth very little in the kingdom of God, and it is not really ours to keep in the first place. Jesus promises there are things of much greater worth than the trifles we entertain ourselves with daily. He is not very clear in this section about the faithful use of wealth—just what those true riches are— but it seems clear that they are connected to the eternal homes mentioned earlier. In Luke 12:33, Jesus told his disciples to sell their possessions, give them to the poor, and as a result, they would gain treasure in heaven. In Luke 14:14, he talked about a repayment for earthly generosity at the resurrection of the just. These seem to parallel Jesus' teaching here. What Jesus refers to as the true riches must be the same as the treasure in heaven and the reward he mentions earlier in Luke.

There are two ways to think about the eternal riches that Jesus talks about here. One is that they are related to our varying degrees of faithfulness. In other words, those who are more faithful stewards of their wealth in this life are entrusted with more in eternity. A second way to think about it is that those who are faithful stewards of their wealth in this life prove themselves worthy of having any treasure at all in heaven. While I do think there is an argument for the idea that we will get different rewards and/or responsibilities based upon our faithfulness (see the parable of the pounds in chapter 19), this particular passage does not address varying amounts of reward, but rather whether we have any at all. If we are not faithful with the little that belongs to another, we will not be given the true riches that will belong to us. The true riches then, at least here, must be the general blessings of the eternal kingdom. Could it be, then, that if we are not generous with the wealth we have now, we will not be given anything else in eternity because we will not be there to receive it?

The best example of the connection between eternal life and treasure in heaven is in Luke 18, when a rich ruler comes to Jesus seeking how to inherit "eternal life." Jesus tells him that if he sells what he has and gives his money to the poor, he will have "treasure in heaven." Jesus seems to equate eternal life with treasure in heaven. He then tells the disciples it is easier for a camel to go through the eye of a needle than for a rich man to enter the kingdom of God. The disciples indicate they understand that Jesus is talking about eternal consequences by asking, "Who then can be saved?" Entering the kingdom of God, eternal homes, eternal life, treasure in heaven, being saved—these are all part of the same package. There are some who might argue that there is a distinction between salvation and eternal reward, in that one could be saved and yet not have much treasure in heaven.[6] But when it comes to how we use our wealth, Jesus does not appear to separate these ideas. The people who are saved have access to treasure in heaven; those who do not have treasure in heaven are not saved. Separating salvation from eternal reward allows for the confusion that we can have salvation and yet still be unfaithful with our wealth. Jesus does not allow for such a distinction.

The promise of these true riches should blow our minds. If worldly wealth is a "little" thing, imagine what treasure in heaven must be like. This world has a lot to offer; it is obvious from creation that God is not an ascetic. The human desire to create and admire things of beauty comes from God. This divine impulse has led to the discovery and creation of some pretty amazing treasures over the past few thousand years. Yet the true riches that Jesus promises us far exceed anything that we have ever seen or heard of on earth. They cannot perish or be consumed, and they are ours forever.

All these worldly pleasures are mere shadows of what awaits us in eternity—not just in heaven, but when heaven and earth are made new. In Revelation 21, John describes his vision of the New Jerusalem as being made of pure gold with walls adorned with jewels. Even the streets are gold. The things we consider so precious will be common building materials. Undoubtedly, he was trying to describe a beauty that defied description. In his vision there is no temple, because God and Jesus are the temple. Their presence permeates everything. Nighttime was a constant threat to ancient cities since it provided cover for clandestine attacks from enemies. But the glory of God lights the entire eternal city so that darkness never falls. After millennia of only seeing a reflection of their creator, the people of God will finally see him face to face. Nothing we know on earth will compare to what we will experience then.

However, the reward for generosity is not only realized in eternity. After their interaction with the rich man, and Jesus' camel and needle parable, the disciples remind Jesus that they have left everything in order to follow him. Jesus comforts them by saying, "Truly I tell you, there is no one who has left house or wife or brothers or parents or children, for the sake of the kingdom of God, who will not get back very much more in this age, and in the age to come eternal life" (Luke 18:29-30). Not only is there a promise of future true riches, there is also a promise that, as we place our trust in God, we will be taken care of in this life. As we leave our biological families and homes for the sake of the gospel we will gain a spiritual family who will take us into their own homes. Jesus had no place to lay his head, but he was continually taken in.

Paul also makes two points that are important in this discussion of faithful use of our wealth. In his second letter

to the church at Corinth, he appeals to them to give generously to the collection he is taking up for the poor believers
back in Jerusalem:

> The point is this: the one who sows sparingly will
> also reap sparingly, and the one who sows bounti-
> fully will also reap bountifully. Each of you must give
> as you have made up your mind, not reluctantly or
> under compulsion, for God loves a cheerful giver.
> And God is able to provide you with every blessing
> in abundance, so that by always having enough of
> everything, you may share abundantly in every good
> work. (2 Cor 9:6-8)

First, our giving must come out of joy and not out of
obligation or guilt. We have freedom over the resources
God has given us. They are not demanded of us. Neither
Jesus nor Paul attempted to establish a communist state
where people lost control over their money. Our giving
must come out of freedom.

Second, as we give, God will entrust us with more, not
just in the next life but in this one as well. Some have misused this passage to mean that as we give, God will give
us greater possessions to keep. I once heard a sermon at
a church where the pastor talked about how he gave away
a five hundred dollar suit and was given a thousand dollar
suit. He gave away a nice car and was given a luxury car.
While generosity was commendable, Paul's point is not
that we give in order to get even better things. Rather, he
says that God will give to us to provide for our needs so
that we can continue to be generous. I have a friend who

runs a company that caps all the salaries of the executives and then gives the rest to the poor. He has said that the more they give, the more money the company makes. God is generous with those who prove themselves generous. George Muller, whose own faithful use of money was remarkable, wrote in his autobiography, "He has not blessed us that we may gratify our own carnal mind but for the sake of using our money in His service and to His praise."[7]

It seems Jesus has no problem appealing to our self-interest. While this may appear less noble or altruistic to some, there is nothing wrong with seeking things of real value. What is condemned in Scripture is the pursuit of those worldly trinkets that distract us from the treasures of the kingdom. By living generously, we are not only seeking what is of ultimate worth, we are also being transformed more and more into the likeness of God. We should have no reason to believe that the generosity we learn here on earth will be useless to us in eternity, even when poverty is brought to an end. By being free with our wealth in this life, we develop the kind of godly character that is perfected in the eternal kingdom.

4

GOD VS. *MAMMON*

No slave can serve two masters; for a slave will either hate the one and love the other, or be devoted to the one and despise the other. You cannot serve God and wealth.

—Luke 16:13

ONE OF THE MOST PROFOUND BOOKS I HAVE READ ON THE TOPic of wealth is Jacques Ellul's *Money and Power*. He offers deep insight into this passage, so I will quote a good deal from him here. One of those insights is that wealth can have spiritual power over us. We like to think that our money is neutral, that it is just a tool to be used for good or for bad. But Ellul's conviction, which comes from this section of Jesus' teaching, is that wealth is not neutral; in fact, it can be demonic.[1]

Again Jesus begins with a general principle: no one can serve two masters. If you try, you will end up loving one and hating the other. Some scholars have speculated that this would have been literally true in first century Palestine. If you were a slave of one master, certainly you could not at the same time be the slave of another master.[2] However, other scholars have countered that it was possible for a slave to work for two separate masters, and that Jesus' point is not that it is impossible to *attempt* to serve two masters, but that you will inevitably end up loving one more than the other.[3] This is especially true if they have different demands and offer different "rewards." In trying to please one, you would displease the other. You would have to choose to please one master over the other.

The main point of this teaching is that God and *Mammon*—two different masters—are opposed to one another. They cannot be served at the same time because they are very different masters who both require complete allegiance. Several things emerge as we reflect on this brief passage. First, Jesus talks about wealth in a way that personifies it.[4] It is not an object but a presence, one that has the ability to vie with God; one that acts and requires service. Second, it is in conflict with God. Far from neutral, it acts in defiance of God and leads people away from him. This is true because, third, it offers a different life—one that is based upon human effort rather than grace. And fourth, if we attempt to serve both God and *Mammon*, we will end up denying God. Let me explain each of these concepts a bit.

Wealth as a Power

It may be difficult to think of wealth as an entity, or a "power," as Ellul puts it.[5] It is, after all, made from human-made material. It is no more a god than a rock or a tree or a statue. But idols are simply physical objects with spiritual power ascribed to them. We ascribe power to money in the same way. It has no value aside from what we put into it.[6] The paper money we possess, gold, diamonds, houses—these are only material things. We invest them with value and, therefore, with power. Ellul says, "Power is something that acts by itself, is capable of moving other things, is autonomous (or claims to be), is a law unto itself, and presents itself as an active agent."[7] Just like an idol, wealth has no real power unless we give it power, but once we do, it becomes a spiritual reality. Perhaps this is why Luke chose to transliterate the Aramaic word *Mammon* instead of finding one that represented the idea of wealth in Greek. It is as if he is naming *Mammon* as one of the false gods, like Baal, Athena, or Zeus.

A while ago, I was in Cambodia and had a chance to visit Angkor Wat, which is a very impressive complex of temple ruins in the north. Our guide took some time to explain the religious beliefs of the Cambodian people. "Officially," he said, "I am a Buddhist. But our history is rooted in animism. So I feel free to pray to any rock or tree." At first I thought that his idolatry was a bit ridiculous. How can you really petition a rock and think it can do anything for you? But we often do the same with our wealth; we give it power by believing it can help us, make us happy, or protect us. In doing so, our wealth goes from something inanimate to a living, spiritual reality. This is why Paul on two occasions emphasizes that greed is idolatry (Eph 5:5, Col 3:5). It is the worship of another god.

Paul gives another example of this dynamic—giving power to something that then has power over us—in Galatians 4:8-10, where he reminds the church that, as pagans, they once were in bondage to the "elemental spirits." They had become followers of Christ, but then wanted to follow parts of the Jewish Law. Paul likened this to a return to serving these "elemental spirits." The Law was not demonic, of course, but trusting in it apart from the grace of Christ made it a tool of these elemental spirits. The same thing happens with *Mammon*.

Opposition to God

Jesus tells us that we cannot serve both God and *Mammon*. The spiritual power that wealth has is in opposition to God, which means there is something inherently evil about it. In this passage, Jesus calls it "dishonest *Mammon*"—literally, "*Mammon* of iniquity."[8] Ellul concludes that this "means both that *Mammon* generates and provokes iniquity and that *Mammon*, symbol of unrighteousness, emanates from iniquity."[9] In Luke 16, the word "dishonest" is used repeatedly. It is used to describe the manager in the parable; Jesus taught that those who are dishonest with a little will be dishonest with much; and finally, it is used twice to describe wealth. He draws a stark contrast between that which is dishonest and that which is faithful, that which is unrighteous and evil with that which is righteous and true. To Jesus, it is quite clear which side *Mammon* belongs to.

Jesus was not alone in recognizing the demonic force present in *Mammon.* Paul concluded that the love of money is the root of *all* evils (1 Tim 6:10). James saw it as the source of all fighting and wars (Jas 4:1-3). John described the Great Whore of Babylon (symbolic of Rome) as rich, clothed in purple and scarlet, and adorned with gold and jewels and pearls (Rev 17:4); he described her as living luxuriously (18:7) and a consumer of all things fine and extravagant (18:11-13).[10] The belief that wealth is a blessing from God has no foundation in the New Testament; such a case might be made from the Hebrew Bible, but only in a very limited sense.[11] Jesus clearly believes that wealth is inherently in conflict with God.

Mammon's Other Gospel

The reason for this conflict is that *Mammon* sets itself up as an alternative to God. It deceptively promises us the same things God does—namely, provision, safety, happiness, and hope for the future—though it is not actually able to fulfill those promises. Even though we know that wealth is tied to this world and will fail us, its allure is still great because it represents another "gospel." *Mammon* preaches a gospel based upon what we are able to accomplish and control under our own strength. It is a message of self-justification based upon merit.

The writer of Proverbs cries out, "Give me neither poverty nor riches . . . or I shall be full, and deny you, and say,

'Who is the LORD'" (Prov 30:8-9). The wealthy person is tempted to believe that God is not necessary. Ellul says, "God gives riches in creation and we seize them and make them our own; instead of giving glory to God, we glorify ourselves. Sheltered by our riches, we quickly mistake ourselves for God."[12] Wealth is something we have some control over; therefore, we might believe we do not need to trust God if we can trust in what we can accumulate on our own. In this way, as Ellul points out, we become our own gods.

Wealth can also make us feel justified. We might believe we are better than others because of what we have accomplished, what we have acquired, or the lifestyle we have. The world seems to operate under the belief that the rich are more important than others. Why else is the world so fascinated with the rich and famous? Wealth is a sign of success and merit, and our personal value is often wrapped up in our status, which is built upon our incomes, possessions, and lifestyles.

Wealth makes us feel better about ourselves. How many of us have gone shopping not because we need something, but just because it makes us happy? Maybe we were somewhat depressed and the new pair of shoes made us feel better. Spending can be a way to cope with the difficulties of life. Personally, when I am anxious about money I am sometimes *more* tempted to spend it on something frivolous. We may use spending as a way to mask deeper issues of anxiety, grief, or pain. Rather than turning to God, we take matters into our own hands and try to buy relief. Rather than looking to the true Comforter, we seek comfort in material things.

At its core, *Mammon* represents a meritorious worldview. It is opposed to grace because it is fundamentally about what can be earned and purchased.[13] It is enticing to us because our hearts are predisposed toward merit. In Galatians, Paul accuses the church of deserting God and turning to another gospel (Gal 1:6). As the situation unfolds, we realize that the problem is not that they are turning to another god or doctrine, but that some of the Gentiles in the church have been convinced by other Jewish Christians that they need to uphold portions of the Law, most notably circumcision, in order to be saved into the family of God.[14]

Paul's great theological (and missiological) insight was that by adding circumcision to the requirements of following Jesus, the Galatian church was trying, in effect, to earn their salvation through their own efforts instead of trusting God's grace. Jesus had accomplished everything they needed to be reconciled to God, but by their actions, they were proclaiming that Jesus' death was not enough to save them. It was a rejection of the idea that Jesus' blood alone covered their sin.[15] What would make a bunch of Gentile converts *want* to get circumcised? One would think that they would be resistant to such a suggestion, but the lure of self-justification is great and can even lead us to harm ourselves. Our flesh desires to trust in what we can do rather than the grace of God. In fact, it is such a deep part of our nature that we seek out ways to justify ourselves without even consciously trying; I doubt the Galatians thought they were turning to another gospel until Paul pointed it out.

In the same way, trusting *Mammon* denies the cross of Christ. It affirms that we are adequate without God and that we can rely on our own abilities. We use wealth to convince ourselves that we are all right—maybe even better than others. It masks our weaknesses and covers our problems. One of the things I have found while living in a poorer community is that poorer people tend to be much more honest about their own weaknesses than wealthier people. For example, during one of the first conversations I had with one of my new neighbors, she told me her husband drank too much. There was no desire to hide the problem.

I was reflecting recently on the passage in Luke 18 where a blind beggar heard that Jesus was passing by and cried out for mercy. The people tried to shut him up, but he cried out all the louder for mercy until Jesus heard him and had the blind man brought to him. Jesus healed the man, and the man in turn followed him, glorifying God. What struck me most is how in touch the blind man was with his suffering. He did not care that other people told him to be quiet. He did not care that he was socially insignificant. He wanted healing and gave no consideration to what others thought of him. Those who are honest about their suffering are more likely to seek help, and if they have few material resources to depend on, they are more likely to turn to God. However, wealthy people are more tempted to use their wealth to cover their pain and emptiness. Wealth allows the rich to hide their problems—even from themselves.

The gospel of *Mammon* is based upon scarcity. We hoard because we fear there will not be enough, that resources are finite. *Mammon* puts us in competition with our neighbor. We do not see neighbors, then, as brothers and sisters who are part of our communal family, but as competitors. If they take from us, we will be left with less. This may have been one of the concerns of the older brother in Luke 15. He complained his sinful brother was getting the fatted calf when he never received even a young goat; perhaps he was worried that the younger brother would eat into his own future inheritance now that he was back. His labor in the field may also have been motivated by this fear—he was building toward future security, insuring his inheritance.

Since wealth can never really provide us with the security our hearts desire, we are constantly filled with anxiety. Walter Brueggemann writes, "The self-sufficient person knows deep down that self-securing, and self-satisfaction finally are unachievable, because they represent life in a world where no gifts are given. The outcome of such autonomy without allies or support is an endless process of anxiety, for one never has enough or has done enough to be safe and satisfied."[16]

In contrast to *Mammon*, we see in the prodigal son parable that God's resources are not finite. We do not have to labor anxiously after them as if we were servants in the household; he has made us children, and we are entitled to the abundance of his house.

I have some Filipino friends who are part of a large extended family, and despite their size—there are over one hundred descendants of one set of grandparents—they think very collectively. If one family needs money to buy a house, other families will pool their resources to help them. There is a presumed responsibility to the other family members. Brothers and sisters, nieces and nephews, are not considered competitors, nor are they considered drains upon the family. *Mammon* strives to put us into competition for limited resources, but grace assures us that God's resources are unlimited. *Mammon* teaches us that the other person is a threat to our hard-earned possessions, but the Father shows us that we are interconnected, bonded together as siblings by our adoption as sons and daughters.

Denying God

As a spiritual reality, *Mammon* is constantly tempting us to believe in it, to serve it like a god.[17] It desires our hope and our love. In Luke 12, Jesus warns his disciples that where their treasure is, there will be their hearts also—not the other way around. Jesus does not say, where your heart is, there your treasure will be. We deceive ourselves into believing that we can have wealth as long as we do not put our trust in it.[18] This is a great lie. What Jesus says is that if you have wealth you *will* put your trust in it; you will be enticed to serve it. You can store up treasure in heaven or on earth, and wherever that treasure is, *that* is where your heart will be. We cannot serve two masters; if we build up wealth in this life, we will come to despise God by choosing to follow another gospel.

Mammon and God represent two very different worldviews. One is based upon selling and the other upon giving.[19] One is founded upon what can be earned and the other upon grace. If we seek to serve *Mammon*, we ultimately deny God and his Gospel. The only way to break the spiritual power of *Mammon* is to use it counter to its meritorious intentions. Simply put, we must give it away.[20] Using *Mammon* as a tool of grace, of generosity, strips it of all its power to justify. Giving it away breaks any trust we have in it to save and comfort us. When we spend it lavishly upon our poor brother or sister, it becomes a means of grace by providing for their needs.

Mammon covets our worship. It begs us to store it up and keep it safe. It tempts us to believe it alone is able to provide the kind of security and joy we seek. It promises us that we can be the masters of our own fate if we will choose to put our trust in it. Because of this, *Mammon* cannot tolerate generosity. Generosity undermines the very foundation it is built upon. By using our wealth in the faithful way Jesus has described, we exorcize the demonic force bound up with *Mammon,* and it becomes an instrument of the kingdom of God. Generosity is not only the result of trusting God and denying *Mammon*, it is also the means by which we trust God. It is not enough to say we trust God; we demonstrate our trust by our faithfulness with *Mammon*. If we continue to hold onto it, *Mammon* retains its power.

This point that people cannot serve both God and *Mammon* is the culmination of Jesus' teaching in chapter 16 so far. Let me do a quick summary. The parable of the shrewd manager was told to encourage his followers to be wise with their wealth. Instead of storing up wealth on earth, we should use it to bless the poor and thereby invest in eternity. Worldly wealth is a little thing compared to what God offers, but it is a test of faithfulness. If we are generous with it, we will be proven worthy of true, eternal riches. Finally, our desire to hold onto wealth can draw us away from God because God and *Mammon* are in opposition. *Mammon* actively tempts us to worship it by putting our hope in it. When we are stingy with our brothers and sisters, we are endangering our relationship with God because we are denying his grace to us and because greed is, at its root, idolatry. It is impossible to serve both God and *Mammon*, and so, Jesus encourages us, we have to pick a side.

In Mark 4, Jesus tells a parable about a sower. He explains that the seed falls on different kinds of soil, producing different kinds of growth. In one type of soil, the seed grows yet is choked out by weeds and produces no fruit— it is of no use to the farmer. These are the people who hear the word of God but "the cares of the world, and the lure of wealth, and the desire for other things come in and choke the word, and it yields nothing" (Mark 4:19). They believe they are responding to the word, but their desire for wealth makes bearing fruit impossible.

This is an important reality for the American church to wrestle with. Christianity still has a significant presence in American culture, especially when you compare it to other Western nations. And yet its fruitfulness is muted by our unchecked consumption. The economic crisis of the past decade was directly related to our society's greed. We cannot lay the blame solely at the feet of the financial industry, or any other entity for that matter, because we have all accepted a worldview rooted in lust for more possessions. Our culture does not understand contentment. People have cut back on their spending during this economic downturn only because they have had to; the idea that someone would simplify his or her lifestyle in order to be more generous is almost inconceivable. We believe that the quest for a comfortable life is an inalienable right.

We need to reflect regularly on our consumption. If the fires of the American church die down like they have in other nations, I fear it will be because we have grown spiritually fat and immobile. It will be because we continue to feed our avarice at the expense of the poor. It will not be terrorism or war or the liberal and/or conservative agendas that lead to our demise; we will fall under the weight of our own self-indulgence. And as long as we avoid the subject of the dangers of wealth on Sunday, we risk planting seeds that cannot bear real fruit. We will make disciples who believe they are following Jesus, but may, in fact, have chosen another gospel.

Luke tells the stories of two rich men in his narrative.

The first is in chapter 18; here, the rich man is only identified as a "ruler." The other is in the beginning of chapter 19; the rich man is a tax collector named Zacchaeus. The ruler, who was likely a leader in the synagogue, came to Jesus to find out how to inherit eternal life.[21] It is no small thing that a religious person of such stature would come to Jesus to find out how to be saved. Certainly he must have had some ideas himself, but his earnest desire for eternal life led him to the feet of Jesus.

Jesus told him to follow the commandments not to commit adultery, kill, steal, and bear false witness, and to honor his father and mother. The man replied that he had done all these things since his youth. Jesus replied, "There is still one thing lacking. Sell all that you own and distribute the money to the poor, and you will have treasure in heaven; then come, follow me" (Luke 18:22). When Jesus had said this, the ruler became sad because he was very rich. This was a cost he had not anticipated. Jesus then taught his disciples that it is easier for a camel to go through the eye of a needle than for a rich man to enter the kingdom of God. In other words, it is impossible. Initially this teaching surprised the disciples because it seemed that this man was rich because of God's blessing. "Then who can be saved?" they asked. If the righteous rich cannot be saved, who can?

We are often quick to qualify this story of the rich ruler. Some people say this command is only given to one person in the gospels and therefore should not be considered normative for Jesus' followers. But this is not entirely accurate. In Luke 12:33, Jesus tells his disciples to sell their possessions and give to the poor so that that they will have treasure in heaven. And during this interaction with the ruler in chapter 18, his disciples remind Jesus that they have done just that. This command was not just for the rare individual who had a unique struggle with greed; Jesus' closest followers were called to leave everything regardless of whether they struggled with materialism or not. Being free of possessions gave them the liberty to follow Jesus wherever he went and to preach the gospel to the ends of the earth.

On the other hand, it is also true that not *every* follower was commanded to give up all they had. Many of Jesus' followers continued to possess homes. Mary and Martha, for example, welcomed him into their home, and he never condemned them for not leaving everything behind (Luke 10:38-42). They faithfully used their resources for hospitality and to support Jesus' mission. This means we cannot be formulaic in our application of this text. We cannot say that all Christians must sell all they have in order to follow Jesus. But neither can we assume that, as disciples of Jesus, we will not be called to give everything away.

The text does not tell us that the rich man refused to sell everything and follow Jesus, but the point that Jesus seems to draw from the ruler's response is that he is choosing his possessions over eternal life. The rich have a hard time entering the kingdom because their possessions get in the way.

We have a staff couple in Servant Partners, Chris and

Maureen Hodge, who at one time lived a comfortable, upper middle-class lifestyle in the United States. When they felt called by God to move into a poor community in Honduras and minister there, they sold their vacation house and gave up their good incomes and lifestyles to live in a shack with no running water. I was always impressed that people who had enjoyed such amenities could leave them behind so completely—they are an unusual case. Not all of us will be called to sell everything we have, but we all must be open to that possibility.

I believe the story of Zacchaeus is meant to contrast with that of the rich ruler. Zacchaeus, like the ruler, was eager to see Jesus. He was, however, a very different kind of rich person. Instead of someone who might be perceived as righteous, he had made his wealth collecting taxes for the Roman occupiers and had been dishonest along the way. In fact, he likely oversaw a number of tax collectors, making him even more contemptible.[22]

Although Luke does not tell the reader what it was, something compelled Zacchaeus to see Jesus. He was so anxious to get a glimpse of this teacher who befriended tax collectors like himself that he climbed a tree to see him. Such behavior must have been beneath a man with such wealth and authority, but Zacchaeus' desire to see Jesus was greater than his desire to appear respectable. Seeing him up in the tree, Jesus invited himself to Zacchaeus' house for dinner. The crowd responded the same way the Pharisees had in chapter 15; they showed their contempt that Jesus was going to be the guest of a sinner. The stories of these two men—Zacchaeus and the ruler—play out very similarly to the parable of the prodigal son. There are two sons of Abraham. One, Zacchaeus, has become an outcast, while the other, the ruler, is the model of holiness. But in the end, it is the outcast who appreciates the father and does what is right.

In contrast to the ruler, Zacchaeus willingly declared that he would give away half of all his goods to the poor, and that if he had defrauded anyone, which apparently he had, he would repay them four times the amount he had taken, which was more than the Law required (Lev 6:1-5). He did not repent of being a tax collector, and Jesus never called him to stop being one. He distributed half of his justly earned wealth to the needy and used much of the other half to make restitution to the people he had oppressed. Both of these are acts of repentance. He was not just *willing* to give up his wealth; he actually gave it up, or at least most of it. After Zacchaeus' decision to redistribute his possessions, Jesus declared that salvation had come to his house.

Though he was rich, Zacchaeus was one of the lost. He had sinned by oppressing his Jewish brothers and sisters, and he had become an outcast as his profession was judged to be sinful whether or not he worked honestly. His desire for wealth led him to betray his people and oppress the vulnerable. He was aware that he had left the Father's house. In contrast, the ruler believed he was a good, religious person, but his self-righteousness blinded him to the danger of wealth and his need for God.

Any of us can become lost if we try to serve *Mammon*. We should, therefore, never condemn those we consider rich; they are not our enemies. Even those who oppress others should be seen as part of the family. They, too, need to be restored to the Father. Since those of us who are middle-class are truly rich when we consider the distribution of wealth in the world, this is good news; though we may be lost, we can be found. Jesus desires that we be restored to the rest of our family. But restoration requires repentance, and repentance is not merely feeling bad about what we have done. It requires taking steps to change our lives. We have to repent of the ways we have given ourselves to *Mammon*.

Wealth has a powerful grip on American Christians. Too many of us unwittingly believe we can serve God and *Mammon* at the same time. We cannot. Too many of us believe the gospel of Jesus and the gospel of wealth are not at odds. They are. Too many of us believe God is unconcerned about our lifestyles, and some of us believe our wealth is actually a sign of his blessing. But it is easier for a camel to go through the eye of a needle than for a rich person to enter the kingdom of God. That does not mean there is no hope for the rich. As Jesus proclaimed to his disciples, what is impossible for people is possible for God. The rich can be saved in the way Zacchaeus was saved; God made it possible for him to give up his desires for wealth and return to serving him as the one true God. All things are possible for God, even breaking the power of *Mammon* in our lives.

That is very good news. We do not have to be slaves to wealth; we do not need to live under the oppression of working endlessly for something that is ultimately unsatisfying. Once we realize that *Mammon* is not our friend but rather a cruel master who wants to separate us from God, we can choose to leave its care and return home to our good Father.

5

THE PHARISEES' SELF-JUSTIFICATION

*The Pharisees, who were lovers of money, heard all
this, and they ridiculed him. So he said to them, "You
are those who justify yourselves in the sight of others;
but God knows your hearts; for what is prized by human beings is an abomination in the sight of God."*

—*Luke 16:14-15*

ALTHOUGH THE PHARISEES WERE NOT JESUS' INTENDED AUDI-
ence, they had been listening in on his teaching—and it
did not sit well with them. There is no question that they
understood what Jesus was talking about, but they were
not open to being challenged on the topic of wealth because, as Luke tells us, they were lovers of money. In their
theology, God and *Mammon* were not in tension.[1] They
believed that wealth was a blessing from God for a righteous life, and so they scoffed at Jesus' teaching. Is it not
often the case that when we disagree with what is be-

ing said—when it hits too close to home—we attack the source instead of wrestling with the issue? That is exactly what the Pharisees did. Instead of reflecting on how the power of *Mammon* might have adversely affected their relationship with God, they ridiculed Jesus.

A while ago I was teaching a segment of the Perspectives on World Mission course at an affluent church in southern California. I challenged people to think about how they could change their lives to care for the poor. I told them that for some of them it might mean relocating to poorer neighborhoods in the United States or abroad so that they could have more contact with the poor. I was clear that not everyone was called to do so, but that they should at least take the issue to God in prayer. One gentleman raised his hand and said, "Obviously, I am not going to do that, but are there some other ways that I could be in relationship with the poor?" While glad that he felt an increased desire to relate to the needy, I was troubled that questioning his lifestyle was "obviously" not an option. I cannot say with authority that God was speaking to him through me, but I can say that if he was, the gentleman, at least at that moment, was not open to listening.

If our hearts are open to listening, we will find that God is always speaking to us. The Pharisees, however, were not open; their love of money plugged up their ears. I would like to think that if Jesus were the guest preacher at an affluent American church and said the same things he said to his disciples in this text, he would be taken seriously. But would he?

Because of the Pharisees' response, Jesus decided to confront them directly. Their problem, he said, was that they only cared about their image in front of others. God was not fooled, however, by outward appearances. He knew the reality of their hearts. We have seen a theme of self-justification in previous discussions. The older son, for example, justified himself by his slaving away for the father, and we discussed how *Mammon* is, at its core, based upon a meritorious system that allows people to justify themselves. Here, Jesus gives us a new insight into this dynamic. Self-justification is usually about trying to look good before other people, rather than God. The Pharisees presented themselves to others as more righteous than those around them.

In Luke 18, Jesus tells a parable about a tax collector and a Pharisee. They both went to the temple to pray. Jesus says that the Pharisee, praying to *himself*, thanked God that he was not like other people: "Thieves, rogues [the same Greek word we have been translating as "dishonest"], adulterers, or even like this tax collector" (Luke 18:11). The Pharisee fasted twice a week and gave tithes of all he got. The tax collector, by contrast, acknowledged his sin in his prayer and, simply and sincerely, asked God for mercy. Jesus said that the tax collector was the one who went away justified.

The Pharisees thought they were righteous based on how they compared to others. We can always find people who are worse than we are. Whenever we might feel bad about ourselves or about our lack of holiness, it is always comforting to think of those more godless than we. The Pharisees, ultimately, were not trying to do God's will; they were just trying to be better than everyone else, as if God graded on the curve. They were less concerned about what God thought of them than what people thought of them. I imagine they separated everyone into two camps: those who were "sinners" and those who were "righteous"—like they were. How easily we can all get stuck in that trap. We can convince ourselves that we are "righteous" because of the people who are "worse" than we are. Having the "correct" morality, values, theology, and political agenda can convince us that we are good people—even better people. Being around others who share those values reinforces that feeling of superiority.

But God knows our hearts, and we cannot fool him. As Jesus says in this text, the things we prize as humans are abominations to him. As humans, we often desire to be held up publicly as special, unique, or gifted. We seek out things that we believe will make us better than others. Advertisers understand this human impulse very profoundly; they play upon our desires to compare ourselves favorably to others and continually tell us that our worth is tied to what car we drive, what clothes we wear, how young we look, and even how clean our homes are. Some might blame them for making our culture so shallow, but they only tell us what we want to hear—that by purchasing their product we will become better people. Our models for "better" are the young, the beautiful, the rich, the successful, the famous, and the powerful. Such people grace the pages of our magazines, appear in our commercials and movies, and permeate the Internet.

I would like to say that such dynamics are not part of Christian culture, but they are. Often the people that get held up as Christian examples are admired because of their charisma, the size of their churches or ministries, the number of books they write, their connection to important political leaders, and their success in business or sports or entertainment—things that are not bad in and of themselves, but have nothing to do with the values of the kingdom of God. Christians often import the values of the world into the church, making it difficult for Christian leaders to be successful unless they are successful in a worldly sense. We are tempted, then, to present ourselves as righteous, even when we are struggling.

Years ago, I was part of a prayer ministry team at a large Christian gathering. A woman, probably in her sixties, came to me for prayer. She and her husband had had difficulty in their sex life for years, and she wanted to finally confess the conflict to someone and seek wisdom from God about how to move forward. She confessed to me that her husband had resisted counseling because he held a significant role in a Christian organization and was afraid of what people might think of him. He had not wanted her to even seek prayer for fear their issues would be made known. He was willing to let his marriage suffer in order to keep up the appearance of righteousness.

This is precisely the sin of the Pharisees. The Pharisees prized being separate, being better, and their wealth was part of what made them so. They probably even viewed it as a reward for their superior righteousness, an outward sign of their internal holiness.[2] We may not admire Christians simply because they are wealthy, but we do associate wealth with success and importance. Some churches even give their pastors luxury cars and houses as a sign of the generosity of the congregation and the worth of the pastor. As the director of a non-profit, I can tell you it is tempting to treat the large donors differently than the small ones. A larger gift means a larger percentage of your budget. You begin to think that if you can just secure that gift, you will be taken care of. So those donors become more important. Larger givers get treated differently.

This is not a new problem. James warned his congregations about favoring the rich:

My brothers and sisters, do you with your acts of favoritism really believe in our glorious Lord Jesus Christ? For if a person with gold rings and in fine clothes comes into your assembly, and if a poor person in dirty clothes also comes in, and if you take notice of the one wearing the fine clothes and say, "Have a seat here, please," while to the one who is poor you say, "Stand there," or, "Sit at my feet," have you not made distinctions among yourselves, and become judges with evil thoughts? (Jas 2:1-4)

When we treat people differently based on their large giving we are guilty of making the same distinctions that James condemned.

In Luke 21, as Jesus watched people putting their gifts

into the temple treasury, he called attention to the poor widow who put in two copper coins. She had put in more than all the rest, he said, because they had given out of their wealth but she out of her poverty gave everything she had. From God's perspective, those who have fewer resources but give more of it away, are more generous than those who give out of their abundance. How often do we see that value praised in the world or even the church?

For most of us who have grown up immersed in American values, there is a part inside of us that believes wealth makes us better people. It is a heart dysfunction, not merely a cultural one. On one of my first visits to a squatter community in Manila, I was talking to one of the residents about his desire to buy a house. He said it would cost him the equivalent of about ten thousand dollars. I asked if he was able to get a loan for that amount, and he told me that such credit was not available to people in his community. He asked me if Americans had such resources and, without thinking, I pulled out a credit card with a ten thousand dollar limit and observed that it could pay for a house. He seemed amazed and impressed that such a small thing could hold such power. Later, however, I was embarrassed by my actions. I wanted this man to like me, and, subconsciously, I had gotten sucked into wanting to impress him with my wealth (more accurately, my access to debt). It disgusts me to write these words, but such is the grip that *Mammon* has had on me.

Although I have grown through the years to understand more fully the lies of *Mammon*, I must still fight the temptation to believe that wealth makes you more important. When I visit our work in Johannesburg, South Africa, I usually visit a lower middle-class black church on the out-skirts of the squatter community we work in. The pastor is an advocate of what we are trying to do. What has most impressed me is that he never recognizes us before the congregation, although we certainly stick out. One of the members of our team is African American, but the others are white South African and Korean American. I am then the only white American in the room. We do not get asked to preach or give a testimony, nor are we even introduced. He has told us that he wants to treat us just like everyone else in the congregation; we get no special treatment be-cause we are rich or white or American, which I deeply appreciate. He is putting into practice James' instruction.

Trusting in wealth to justify us before other people is an abomination to God. He does not favor people based upon their income, social status, position in the church, worldly accomplishments, amount of donations, or any other form of "righteousness" we may create for ourselves. He sees us for who we really are. Unlike our fellow hu-mans, he knows our thoughts, our motives, and our carnal desires, and despite our appearances, he knows just how righteous and unrighteous we are.

Self-justification can take many forms and is not limited to those who store up wealth. Generosity was a common trait in the early church. In Acts 4, Luke records how peo-ple routinely sold their possessions to care for the needs of the larger community of believers. One of those specifically mentioned was Joseph of Cyprus who sacrificed his own property to provide for others' needs. Perhaps because of this, or because of his general generous nature, the apostles named him Barnabas, meaning "Son of Encouragement."

In Acts 5, Luke tells the story of Ananias and Sapphira immediately after the Barnabas story. Undoubtedly, the couple witnessed the praise that Barnabas received and desired to be exalted in the same way. They, too, sold a piece of land, but held back some of the money they had received. It is unclear why they chose to hold some back, but this was not their sin. Their sin was that they *said* they had given all their profit, thus making themselves appear more sacrificial than they were. When Peter confronted them, he reaffirmed that the money was theirs and they were free to do with it what they wanted; they were not obligated to give the whole sum away. However, deceiving people into believing they were more righteous could not be tolerated. Such deception, had it spread in the new community, would be disastrous. Judgment fell upon them not because they lacked generosity, but because they lied about their generosity in order to win people's praise.

Earlier in this chapter, I cited the parable of the Pharisee who justified himself over the tax collector. One of the things he recorded on his spiritual resume was that he gave tithes of everything he earned. His generosity was part of his self-justification. One of the dangers of the ministry in which I serve is believing that our simplicity makes us righteous. Almost all of our teams have had, at one point, some tensions over what it means to live like the people in the poor community they serve. It is easy to convince yourself that you are more faithful because you do not have as many "luxuries" as other people on the team. I have sometimes believed that my own commitment to working for social justice and living in a simple house in a poorer community makes me a more authentic believer than the average American Christian. But God knows my heart, and our sacrifice does not fool him any more than our success does. If our motivation is to look good before people, the costs we pay for the "sake of the gospel" are worthless. As Paul writes, "If I give away all my possessions, and if I hand over my body so that I may boast, but do not have love, I gain nothing" (1 Cor 13:3).

Paul implies that it is in fact possible to make great sacrifices for the Christian cause with a motivation other than love. Ironically, the quest for justice can lead to great injustice toward our brothers and sisters. Some of the least gracious people I have met are those who have committed their lives to seeking justice in the world. It is, as my wife says, an occupational hazard. Working for justice requires seeing the evil in our world and calling attention to it. It pits those of us who are "right" against those who are "wrong." There is no problem with fighting for what you believe is right, but sometimes we are tempted to believe that right equals good, and wrong equals evil. Thus, we become "good" people fighting, not against evil in the world, but against people we see as evil because they do not share our convictions. Being right makes us feel like we are better.

This attitude is in direct opposition to the kingdom that Jesus proclaims. To enter it, we must acknowledge that we are broken, sinful people who cannot make ourselves right before God or others on our own. In a way, claiming citizenship in the kingdom of God is an admission of failure. We have not earned it by our hard work, nor have we lost it by our past mistakes.

There are a couple of simple ways to test whether we are justifying ourselves by our efforts. If our actions, beliefs, or lifestyles lead us to pass judgment on others as being less faithful or authentic, then we have to examine our motivations. Are we responding to the call of God, or are we joining a righteousness club that excludes the unworthy? Do we let people see our strengths but deceive them about our weaknesses and the limits of our faithfulness? Are we like Barnabas who, out of his experience of God's grace, gave sacrificially without desire for praise? Or are we like Ananias and Sapphira who were motivated by the praise of others and therefore sought to deceive? If judgment and deception live in our hearts, then we have a problem.

However, even the purest motive is flawed. Personally, I know that my motivations for taking steps of faith are always mixed. There is the voice of God and the conviction of sin, but there is also my pride and my desires to be a better Christian than others. Yet the solution to such internal conflict is not inaction, though we could quickly run to that option. The remedy for an imperfect heart is the cross of Christ. His grace can break the power of our flawed motives and free us to love those we are tempted to consider less faithful. It also frees us to stand before others as we are and not only as we would want them to see us. To proclaim the cross is to admit failure and acknowledge imperfection. It is to confess that we are not good enough to earn God's love. We might appear holy, but in our hearts we know that we are at times jealous, hateful, judgmental, selfish, lustful, greedy, ambitious, and fearful, among other things.

In his *Personal Narrative*, Jonathan Edwards recounts how when people came to confess their sins to him he always felt that his own sins were so much more severe.[3] Is *that* not the mark of true righteousness? It is not perfection but the conviction of imperfection that leads to justification, as we saw in Jesus' parable about the tax collector. Such conviction leads us to greater dependency upon the mercy of God. It is when we begin to believe that we are good, and in fact better than other people, that we are in the greatest spiritual jeopardy.

Paul Tournier notes that "the strange paradox present on every page of the Gospels and which we can verify any day, is that it is not guilt which is the obstacle to grace, as moralism supposes. On the contrary, it is the repression of guilt, self-justification, genuine self-righteousness and smugness which is the obstacle."[4] In order to remain found, we have to acknowledge the ways in which we are still lost. To become the new creation that God calls us to—to do justice, love mercy, and walk humbly with the Lord—we need to take an honest look at our hearts.

Those who seek to live lives of justice but who are unwilling to plumb the depths of their own fallenness are on a road that will lead eventually to tragedy.

Money was one of the ways the Pharisees justified themselves, but it was more than simply a personal sin. They created whole systems that reinforced their self-worth and gave them power. Because we rarely see Jesus confronting the Roman occupiers, we could falsely assume that Jesus did not believe in changing the systems of his day, but he was constantly confronting the religious, economic, and political leaders of his day in the Herodians, Pharisees, Sadducees, scribes, and priests. Although they did not have the military and political might of Rome, the religious leaders of his day were very much a part of the systems that governed the daily lives of those living in first century Palestine. As a result, they were able to enrich themselves and keep the vast majority of society poor and powerless.

Robert Linthicum observes:

> The vehicle the Jewish leaders used to control the populace and to maintain this grossly unbalanced economic and political structure was their interpretation of the Mosaic Law. The Pharisees taught the Law to the people, the scribes adjudicated and interpreted the Law, the temple priests conducted public life and the affairs of both the temple and the state under the guidelines of the Law, and the nobility, landowners, and the religious establishment all benefitted from the Law.[5]

Because the Pharisees had the power to teach, interpret, and systematize the implementation of the Law, they were able to use it to benefit their own situation. As we will see more fully in the next chapter, they were able to pick and choose what they wanted the Jewish people to understand and, therefore, do. They conveniently neglected to teach on those passages that would have challenged their wealth and disdain for their poor brothers and sisters.

So when Jesus attacked their self-justification, he was not merely concerned with their individual souls; he was condemning the system they had created that oppressed those who fell outside of their group. They had an obligation as teachers to help people know what God expected of them; instead, they used the Law to bless themselves by holding up things as righteous that were in fact abominations to God. This is why Jesus was such a threat to them and one of the reasons why they wanted him killed. Jesus had not simply offended the Pharisees; he assaulted their whole way of life.

We are not that different from the Pharisees. Many of us have entered into or created similar systems in order to justify ourselves, and our value has become linked to the system's survival. If the system is threatened, we are threatened. You see this over and over again in institutions; when an accusation is made against large systems, the reflex response is to protect the institution rather than deal with the truth of the complaint.

One of the communities we work with overseas has numerous other non-profits and churches serving it. The largest ministry is a community center run by an affluent church in another part of town. Recently, our staff helped a group of young men from the squatter community start a cycling club. The men developed the idea themselves and came up with a name for the club; our staff connected them to resources, and a grant was written to help them buy bicycles and a storage unit to keep them in. The woman who offered to write the grant went to the large non-profit and asked if the club could pursue the grant in their name so that the community center could act as the fiscal agent, a conduit for the money. The men also asked if they could put the storage unit on the non-profit's land. The community center graciously agreed.

However, after the grant was processed and the bicycles and storage unit purchased, the community center declared that the property was now theirs. They agreed that the unspent cash belonged to these men, but that it would be used to cover the storage unit rental fees—fees to store the bicycles that the men no longer had access to because the community center feared the men might steal them. The community center also insisted that the name of their club be changed to the name of the community center. The men were angered and disillusioned, but after several meetings with the director of the community center they decided it was easier to walk away and start over.

What would cause a ministry to so abuse the very people it was there to serve? The answer is simple: money. There is a system in place. This large non-profit has a large budget that it must raise money for, and the community center has to show it has good programs in order to keep funding from people in the church and abroad. The cycling club was a potential funding goldmine and someone had already done the hard work of launching it. From the outside, it is an obvious abuse of power, but I imagine the director of the community center merely saw it as a way to keep the non-profit in the black and able to help more people. The system had to be maintained.

Such is the insidiousness of *Mammon*. It tells us to find value in our own efforts apart from God and leads us to establish systems that reinforce that value. If we are to be free of self-justification, we must wrestle with our own heart conditions and examine the misguided systems we support. We must make sure that our churches, and other Christian bodies, do not institutionalize those values that Jesus finds abhorrent.

6

THE GOOD NEWS
OF THE KINGDOM OF GOD

The law and the prophets were in effect until John came; since then the good news of the kingdom of God is proclaimed, and everyone tries to enter it by force. But it is easier for heaven and earth to pass away, than for one stroke of a letter in the law to be dropped. Anyone who divorces his wife and marries another commits adultery, and whoever marries a woman divorced from her husband commits adultery.

—Luke 16:16-18

MOST OF US REACH SOME POINT, USUALLY LATER IN LIFE, where the mere fact that something is different seems to make it evil. My grandmother hates the new digital thermostat she has and wants me to find an old fashioned mercury one. She routinely decries this confusing technological world with its Internet, which she has a hard time conceptualizing. Speaking of her new phone, my mother-in-law said, "I hate it because it's different than my old one." As we age, change becomes harder. We become used to things working a certain way, and having to learn new systems can be disorienting.

Of course, this is not just limited to the elderly; we can be resistant to change at any age. My daughter was concerned about going into second grade because it would be different and unknown. She had flourished in first grade, but the idea of getting to know a new teacher with a different set of rules caused her more anxiety than excitement. In general, humans become emotionally invested in the comfort of the known system.

Change is particularly hard for those who have succeeded in a given system; if the system changes, their whole advantage is threatened as others might rise up and take away their dominance. There was a ten-year period in college basketball when dunking was banned because they felt it gave an unfair advantage to those who were exceptionally tall (specifically, Lou Alcindor). Can you imagine bringing back such a rule now? Beyond the fact that known systems are more comfortable, many people have a vested interest in preserving the status quo because they benefit from it.

Initially, it might be unclear how verses 16-18 connect with Jesus' larger treatment of wealth in Luke 16. How do the coming kingdom, the Law, and divorce fit into his argument? The apparent disconnect has led some scholars to believe these verses were put here somewhat arbitrarily by Luke.[1] But Jesus was aware that his teaching on *Mammon* was challenging the systems the Pharisees had established based upon their assumptions about God and wealth. He knew they were reluctant to change. In these verses, Jesus explains what about the Law had changed and what had not.

Jesus says that with John's appearance something new had happened. The Law and the Prophets had been the standard for the people of God for hundreds of years, but now the good news of the kingdom of God was being proclaimed. It should not surprise us that the Pharisees were having a hard time adjusting to this shift in power. The kingdom threatened their status and way of life, and it challenged everything they thought they knew about living as God's chosen people. The kingdom had come and Jesus was exposing the lies the Pharisees had built their lives upon—wealth and status.

The concept of God's kingdom was not actually a new idea. In his book *Simply Christian*, N. T. Wright writes:

> *The prophet Isaiah, in line with several Psalms and other biblical passages, had spoken of God's coming kingdom as the time when (a) God's promises and purposes would be fulfilled, (b) Israel would be rescued from pagan oppression, (c) evil (particularly the evil of oppressive empires) would be judged, and (d) God would usher in a new reign of justice and peace. Daniel had envisaged a coming time when the monsters (that is the pagan empires) would do their worst, and God would vindicate his people to*

set everything straight. The world was to be turned
the right way up at last. To speak of God's kingdom
arriving in the present was to summon up that en-
tire narrative, and to declare that it was reaching its
climax. God's future was breaking into the present.
Heaven was arriving on earth.[2]

Jesus' contemporaries largely expected that the
Scriptures Wright references would be fulfilled when the
Messiah restored the kingdom of Israel and brought back
all those who were scattered among the nations.[3] Even
after his death, Jesus' own disciples seemed to hold this
view as they mourned. They had hoped he had been the
one to rescue Israel (Luke 24:21). However, the kingdom
Jesus preached was not limited by geographic, political, or
ethnic/cultural lines. His kingdom would not be established
by a military revolution that overthrew the oppressing nation. His kingdom would be established because of his
self-sacrifice on the cross. It was a revolution of a different
sort, far grander than anyone had imagined. Wright continues, "The time had now come when, at last, God would
rescue his people, and the whole world, not from mere
political enemies, but from evil itself, from the sin which
had enslaved them."[4]

Jesus came to liberate people in the fullest sense and
to create a new civilization of freed people. In his first sermon recorded in Luke, Jesus announced that his coming
fulfilled the words from Isaiah 61:1-2: "The spirit of the Lord
is upon me, because he has anointed me to bring good
news to the poor. He has sent me to proclaim release to

the captives and recovery of sight to the blind, to let the oppressed go free, to proclaim the year of the Lord's favor" (Luke 4:18). This was his kingdom declaration. Many scholars connect these passages in Isaiah and Luke to the Jubilee talked about in Leviticus 25 (which we will look at in more depth later).[5] In that text, every fifty years Israel was commanded to restore to the previous owners land that had been lost. During this Jubilee year, those who had fallen into slavery would be released as well. People were given a chance to start over, to come out of debt and into a new reality. Jesus' kingdom declaration, however, was not just for a year of Jubilee as an application of Leviticus 25, but an entire era of Jubilee fulfilled by the coming kingdom.[6] Those who had been cut out of society—both physically and spiritually—would be given a second chance. They would come out of poverty and slavery into abundance and freedom. In him, all the promises of Jubilee would find their fulfillment.

It can be tempting to spiritualize Jesus' words in Luke 4. One may argue that he did not mean the physically blind but rather the spiritually blind, not the physically poor but the spiritually poor. While Jesus' ultimate work was the liberation and healing of souls, Jesus saw the physical arena as essentially linked to the spiritual. The proof that he was the Messiah was that he ministered to the physical needs of the people as well as to the spiritual. The best evidence for this comes in Luke 7; when John was unsure about whether or not Jesus was the true Messiah, he sent a couple of his disciples to ask him if he was, in fact, the one they had been waiting for: "Jesus had just then cured many people of diseases, plagues, and evil spirits, and had given sight to many who were blind. And he answered them, 'Go and tell John what you have seen and heard: the blind receive their sight, the lame walk, the lepers are cleansed, the deaf hear, the dead are raised, the poor have good news brought to them'" (Luke 7:21-22). Jesus' ministry to the physically and socially broken proved he had come from God; it was evidence that the kingdom had come to earth. Jesus knew that John would recognize the signs of the kingdom and the work of the king.

As I have said, at first glance, Luke 6:16 seems like a strange transition in Jesus' rebuke. The law and the prophets were in effect until John came, and now the kingdom of God is being proclaimed and everyone is storming the gates. The key to understanding how this transition fits into his argument is the word "everyone." Ever since Moses came down from Mount Sinai, the people of Israel had been under the Law. The prophets added their divinely inspired voices to the commandments, and together these were the revelations of God and of his will for his people. But John ushered in a new era. He proclaimed the coming of the one true king who would establish the kingdom of God.

This kingdom opened its doors to those who had been excluded under the era of the Law and the prophets. Jesus controversially welcomed the dregs of society into his kingdom, the very people that the Pharisees were trying to keep out.[7] Now, *everyone* was able to enter.

The idea of people coming in "by force" may confuse us

a little, suggesting maybe that there was some battle to get in, or that the kingdom was trying to fend people off. There is a fair amount of debate about the meaning of this sentence, but I believe that it simply means that people have to exercise considerable effort to enter the kingdom.[8] What was surprising to the Pharisees was that those who were most willing to fight to enter the kingdom were the people they felt were most unworthy of it. The poor and downtrodden had discovered the city of gold, the sinner had discovered a country of grace, and all of them would force their way through the door to this new discovery.

The coming kingdom of God was a direct attack on the Pharisees' system of self-righteousness. If God would accept tax collectors and sinners, the poor and the outcast, then all the things they did to separate themselves from these people meant nothing. They were, in fact, no better than the people they held themselves above. Everyone could come into the kingdom if they wanted to. This refers back to the parable of the lost son. If the younger son, despite the horrible things he had done, could be welcomed back, then the older son's trust in his own hard work meant squat. It had not made him better than his younger brother, or more deserving of reward. Those who seek to justify themselves cannot stand grace, especially when it is extended to people they deem unworthy.

Many years ago, there was an older woman in our church who coordinated all the social functions. She enjoyed the power that this brought, and when we hired a new pastor she sat him down in his office and made sure he understood that she ran the church. Our new pastor, who was Latino, started to invite his family members and Latino friends to our church, and the culture change that ensued, needless to say, did not sit well with this woman. During one church dinner she pulled a Latina woman aside and said, "You know, we never invited you people to come." To her credit, this Latina sister did not lash out at her, but she was deeply pained by the woman's overt prejudice. When she shared this story with a few of us, one of our friends rebuked what had been spoken over her. "We invited you," he assured her. After a short while, the older woman and her husband left the church. Sadly, they just could not handle the kinds of people who were coming.

From the Pharisees' perspective, Jesus welcoming "everyone" into the kingdom implied that he was relaxing the rigorous demands of the Law. The Pharisees had never invited these "sinful" people because they were lawbreakers. It is understandable that they might wonder if the kingdom that Jesus proclaimed was in contradiction to the Law. Was Jesus now saying that the Law did not matter? Such would have been an understandable question, which is why Jesus addresses this issue directly. The kingdom does not nullify the Law, he argues, rather it fulfills the Law because it embodies God's full intention for his people. Jesus assures his listeners that the Law was not being thrown out by stating emphatically that "it is easier for heaven and earth to pass away, than for one stroke of a letter in the law to be dropped." The kingdom did not eliminate the Law; it completed it.

How this is true is not immediately obvious, and so Jesus gives an example of how the kingdom fulfills the Law: "Anyone who divorces his wife and marries another commits adultery, and whoever marries a woman divorced from her husband commits adultery" (Luke 16:18). At first read, this example does not seem to shed any light on his argument; in fact, it seems like a bit of a non sequitur. People at the time, though, likely knew exactly what Jesus was talking about.

Based on Deuteronomy 24:1-4, Jesus' contemporaries believed that the Law allowed a man to get a divorce. In other texts, Jesus argues that Moses' instruction was not so much to bless divorce, as it was to put constraints upon what could become a greater evil because of their hardness of heart (Mark 10:5). Nonetheless, the practice had become accepted despite the debates over the instances when a man was allowed to divorce his wife.[9] Here, Jesus explains the kingdom position, which exceeds the requirements of the Law: divorce is always sin because when a divorced man remarries, or when an unmarried man marries a divorced woman, he commits adultery.[10] Jesus' point is that once you are married you are linked to that person for life. The two have become one. Divorce cannot undo that reality. In Jesus' time, the controversy around divorce and remarriage was not merely moral; it was also political. John the Baptist had confronted Herod about marrying his brother Phillip's former wife and John ended up getting arrested and, eventually, beheaded because of it. Jesus had to know he was affirming John's stance that Herod and his wife had committed adultery.

There are other biblical texts that appear to qualify Jesus' statement on divorce and remarriage here in Luke, as well as in Mark 10:2-9. In Matthew 5:32 and 19:9, Jesus seems to allow for divorce and remarriage if a wife is unfaithful. Paul does not include this exemption when he passes on his understanding of Jesus' teaching, but he does acknowledge that divorce may still happen in the Christian community (1 Cor 7:10-11). However, he argues, if someone gets divorced he or she can avoid the worse sin of adultery by remaining unmarried or being reconciled to his or her spouse.[11] We should not make too much of the qualification in Matthew. The emphasis of the Matthew version is the same as that found in Mark, Luke, and Paul: "To break the marriage union is to fail of God's purpose."[12] Yet these texts do provide a caution that even though divorce is never ideal, we should be careful not to be legalistic in our application of Jesus' teaching. From a pastoral point of view, there may be situations when divorce and/or remarriage are better than remaining married or single, as seen in Matthew 19:9. Jesus has argued strenuously against legalism and condemning anyone because of their sin, and so we have to assume he is not saying in Luke that anyone who is divorced and remarried cannot be forgiven.

But in the text here in Luke, Jesus does not really want to engage a lengthy discussion about divorce, its qualifications, or its political implications. It is an example of how the kingdom fulfills and supersedes the Law. The Law allows for divorce, but that does not mean that divorce is good. Far from doing away with the Law, the kingdom raises the bar higher. His point here is that the righteousness God intends for us far exceeds what is laid out in the Law.

The kingdom is established upon grace, but this in no way eliminates the need for holiness; in fact, it calls for a greater holiness. Donald Bloesch argues this point:

Jesus made it very clear that there is a qualitative gulf between the legal righteousness of Judaic tradition and the higher righteousness of the kingdom of God. Without denying the rightful place of the first, he contended that those who take up the cross in costly discipleship are summoned to a style of life that radically transcends the righteousness of the scribes and Pharisees (Matt 5:17-20). The lesser righteousness is not to commit adultery by union of our bodies; the greater is not to commit adultery in the heart. The lesser righteousness is not to steal; the greater is to renounce the right to reparation for wrongs suffered. The lesser is to forgive when amendment of life is evident; the greater is to forgive unconditionally. The lesser is to love those who can be expected to reciprocate in love; the greater is to love our enemies, to do good and lend, expecting nothing in return. (Luke 6:35)[13]

From the text we have been reflecting on, we could also add that the lesser righteousness is to give alms and tithe our ten percent, but the greater righteousness is to give sacrificially and to forsake all love of money. In this way, Jesus can rightly say that the Law will never pass away, nor is it invalidated or relaxed by the kingdom.

What we see here is that Jesus cares more about our heart condition than whether or not we are adhering to a certain set of rules. When we base our lives upon trying to uphold a particular law, besides the risk of self-justification, we fall into the danger of testing the line—how close we can get without crossing it. A good friend of mine often says that if sin were a cliff, we would be tempted to see just how close we can get to the edge before falling off. Children are the masters of this philosophy; they seek how far they can go before their parents rein them in. This may be natural in children as they explore their boundaries, but most of us never seem to grow out of our childish ways. We push God to see how far we can stray before he "punishes" us. Since God rarely confronts us as dramatically as he did Paul on the road to Damascus, we can go pretty far over the cliff before we realize we are falling.

Instead of asking what the minimum requirement for righteous living is, we should seek to have our hearts formed into what God wants them to be. If we understand that sin is death, we should want to get as far away from its edge as possible. This is Jesus' challenge to the Pharisees. They held to the Law so rigidly even to the point of adding obligations to insure they did not break it, but their hearts had strayed from God. Instead of seeking God's full intention for them, they focused on a set of rules that served to assure them of their justification. They held to the letter of the Law, but missed the spirit. And, as we will see, their self-justification led them to miss a bunch of the letters as well.

In the kingdom, Jesus is not merely trying to constrain or elicit a particular behavior; he wants our hearts to be transformed. This is a much higher expectation than holding to a particular set of rules; it is also more complicated. It would have been easier to obey if Jesus had said we cannot own a Mercedes if we want to follow him, rather than asking us to free our hearts from servitude to *Mammon*. With this higher expectation, it is harder to justify ourselves; God knows our hearts and our motivations, and we cannot deceive him—or ourselves—with our actions if our hearts are not in the right place. Nor can we pass judgment on others since, despite their actions, we can never really know what is happening in their hearts. Only God sees everything.

Jesus is calling us to live as citizens of the kingdom of God—a citizenship determined not by where we live, but by how we live. This means first and foremost that we, as the people of God, are to live under God's rule. When many people immigrate to the United States, they retain much of their home country culture, laboring to keep some of their key traditions and values alive even if they are radically different from those of their new country. In a similar way, citizens of the kingdom are to live as if they have a distinct culture. Our traditions, values, and worldview are different from those of this fallen world in which we have made our home. But here is where the analogy breaks down: unlike immigrants to a new country, our true culture does not lie behind us, but before us. Instead of trying to preserve aspects of what we left behind, we are called to become more culturally like our future country that is awaiting the day when it will be fully established.

It is important that we do not confuse our eternal kingdom home with heaven. Scripture teaches that these are different, and that difference affects how we understand our relationship with the kingdom in this life. Jesus instructs us to pray for God's kingdom to come on earth because the earth, not heaven, is our true home.[14] In Revelation 5:10, the four living creatures and the twenty-four elders in heaven sing a new song to Jesus, proclaiming that he is worthy of praise because he has purchased people from all over the earth with his blood and has made them into a kingdom of priests to serve God and to reign *on earth*. Jesus not only died for people so that they could be saved, he died for them so that they could be formed into a new nation that would, one day, rule over all the earth. For the past two thousand years, Jesus has been building a people committed to his kingdom. When the appointed time comes, those people will take over leadership of the world and the Lord's Prayer will finally be fulfilled: "Your kingdom come, your will be done, on earth as it is in heaven" (Matt 6:10).

If we are to be among those who reign in his kingdom when it is fully established on earth, we must prepare ourselves by becoming good citizens now. This means that our hearts need to embrace God's culture of generosity. We need to forsake the love of money and self-justification and become a people of grace. We need to care for the poor and the oppressed and seek justice in the world. We need to realize that the kingdom is open to all people—even those whom we may feel are unworthy of it.

The kingdom has tremendous potential to impact believers in radical ways. There is a book, now out of print, called *Through the Valley of the Kwai*. The author, Ernest Gordon, a British soldier, relates the story of his imprisonment in a Japanese POW camp in Thailand during WWII. Gordon tells how the Japanese guards were exceedingly cruel and that, because of this, many of the men died from malnutrition, disease, and abuse. Yet amidst all the disease and suffering something extraordinary happened: a revival broke out. Soldiers started becoming Christians or rediscovering their faith. They did not just hold Sunday services; they started living fully in the kingdom. They served and loved each other, even laying down their lives for one another.

Gordon recounts how, on one occasion, the Japanese guards found that a shovel was missing after a work party returned. The guards threatened to kill every man in the work party one by one until the guilty party took responsibility. One man stepped forward and was quickly executed. It was discovered later that the shovels had been miscounted and none was missing. The executed man had given his life to save everyone else.

These prisoners bound each other's wounds and gave what little food they had to the sick. Gordon found that those who lived only for their own survival did not survive long, but those who sacrificed for others thrived despite the conditions. These redeemed men even came to forgive the guards for their mistreatment. Most remarkably, when they were finally liberated by the British military, they saved the Japanese guards from death at the hands of the British soldiers, who were enraged at the condition in which they found their countrymen.

Gordon and his compatriots discovered the joy of the kingdom in one of the worst situations imaginable. Sadly, when they returned home they found that the church did not look like the kingdom they had experienced. I imagine many of us can relate to this in some way. Often, the church does not appear to be an institutional manifestation of the kingdom, but rather like the ruins of a once great civilization. This is not new for the people of God. Throughout history, women and men have had to rediscover the kingdom in the midst of institutions that seem to have forgotten it. That rediscovery always begins in our hearts with a work of the Holy Spirit. What Gordon and the other soldiers experienced in the POW camp was the kingdom as Jesus proclaimed it—the one the downtrodden were fighting their way into.

The kingdom not only affects the way the people of God live, it also brings us into conflict with the systems of the world. Since the dawn of civilization, the wealthy have used their money to gain power and the powerful have used their position to gain money. Like we saw with the Pharisees in the previous chapter, the wealthy and powerful create systems that protect their ways of life and rage against any effort that challenges those systems. This is not a socialist or communist analysis, but a spiritual one. These characteristics are the result of *Mammon*'s system of government, just as servant leadership, self-denial, and neighborly love are marks of the kingdom's presence.

Our ministry in Mexico City has encountered a political party that claims to represent the poor. In fact, they do fund many community projects and lend money to build houses at very low interest, but there are always strings attached. In order to qualify for their programs, residents have to show up to a certain number of political rallies. Sometimes people are required to vote for specific candidates and are told to prove their votes with photos from their cell phone cameras. Thousands of people are beholden to this party. This keeps them in power and allows them to deliver votes to their parent party, the PRI, which is the current Mexican president's party.

At times, when our people have worked with residents to improve their community, this party has solved the problem before anyone else could begin to help. Their power is based on the people's poverty and dependence on them, so the political party cannot risk anyone else helping the poor. At first this may seem like an ideal situation: all you have to do is come up with some desire and the party fulfills it. But the downside is that people in the community are never empowered to take responsibility for their neighborhood. They can never become leaders. The party wants to make sure that the people remain dependent upon them.

There are many systems in the world that directly benefit from poverty. Votes are purchased in slums all around the world. Even in the United States, systems exist to keep some people in power and others out. While they may not be as intentional as the Mexican party's efforts, the effect is the same. And where there is power, there is always money.

I mentioned before how we battled an effort to create a waste transfer station in our city, and in doing so discovered how much money the company had spent to win friends and buy loyalties. Our fight also exposed an inner circle of city leaders, most of whom were business leaders. Some were presidents of universities, some led large nonprofits, and almost all belonged to one service club. The same set of people sat on the boards of all the largest institutions in the city; they went to the same parties and fundraisers; they created a cabal of power players. The brilliance of this waste management company was that, over a ten-year period, they had fully infiltrated this group of leaders.

When we criticized the project, these leaders rallied to the company's side. They said they cared about the project for its merit, though they opposed an identical project by a rival company when it had been proposed earlier. The company responded even more strongly through verbal anger and veiled threats. We were falsely accused of taking money from their competitor, of hiring illegal immigrants to walk through the community to get people to sign petitions, and of lying about their project. The owners of this company were not used to people standing up to them.

We knew the fight was bigger than the waste transfer station. We were fighting for the soul of our city, which had been purchased for a few hundred thousand dollars' worth of charitable donations. We were battling for the right of every person in the community, no matter how poor, to have their voices heard and considered. Many of these city leaders gave to causes that helped the poor, but still they were unwilling to listen to them and treat them as equals. They did not want to learn from the people they were trying to help.

One of the waste company's allies was an old family friend of ours. He approached me one day when I was visiting his church and invited me to a nonprofit banquet where the owner of the company was being honored for his charitable work. He told me that it would improve my reputation with that group of city leaders. I knew he meant well, and I appreciated that he cared about my reputation and desired to have it restored among people he respected. But after thinking about it for a while, I realized that I should not care whether these people respected me or not, whether they loved me or hated me. They were not more important in God's eyes because of their wealth and position, and I did not need to impress them. So I chose not to go.

I would love to tell you some romantic ending to the waste transfer fight. I would love to tell you that the poor and oppressed rallied together and vanquished the evil waste company, who repented and acknowledged we were in the right. However, battles with the systems of this world do not always end cleanly. When we realized the company had the political power to get their facility built one way or another, we decided to press them to make some concessions so that the negative impact would be minimized. We convinced them to reduce the size of the facility by a third, to set up a monitoring system to insure that they stayed in compliance, to eliminate any diesel trucks in or out of the facility, and to create a fund that would be used to enforce the codes for any industrial businesses in that neighborhood that were polluting the community. We did not get everything we wanted, but we won a much better situation for the community.

I must also add that some residents were unhappy that we talked to the company at all. In their minds, the company was demonic and represented all the evil that had been done to them. They hoped, as we did, that we could defeat the project outright. However, the majority of us who had fought for over two years knew that there was nothing more we could do, and that if we did not negotiate specific changes to the project, it would get approved as presented with no mitigations. It was a hard loss, but had we not brought our concrete demands for changes to the company, their project would have been much more de-structive to our community.

As Christians, we are called to pray and work for the coming kingdom. As we do so, we will encounter unjust systems. In the United States, immigrants are often denied basic rights. Ethnic minorities are sentenced to much harsher prison terms than whites. Inner-cities suffer from failing schools. Poor communities bear an unequal share of environmentally hazardous businesses. Where democracy is weaker internationally, the systems are even more destructive for the poor. Political corruption, imprisonment without trial, sex trafficking, and slavery are common experiences for many of our poor brothers and sisters around the world. I believe confronting these systems and proclaiming God's vision for the world is part of loving our neighbors. It is a manifestation of the kingdom in the world and is a witness to the heart of God, but we have to confess that even our best efforts will fall short of God's ideal. There are very few total victories this side of eternity, and the kingdom will never fully come until Jesus returns.

This is why it is so important that we understand that we need to live as citizens of the kingdom despite the fallen nature of the world. When we were accused of various falsities in the trash battle, we could have easily returned the vitriol we received. Instead, we tried to respond with humility, respect, and a desire to continue to work together. Because of God's love for us, we can love people who hate us. My wife Lisa realized that the disrespect and threats from the waste transfer station people and public officials left her bitter. One woman had even threatened her physically. Lisa, feeling convicted to pray for her enemies, wrote down the last names of people she felt anger toward. God spoke to her and told her to write down their first names instead, so that she could pray for them as real people, whom God loved as well.

We have realized that limiting the environmental effects of the waste transfer station was only a small part of the kingdom battle; the much larger issues were the way leaders in our city continually attacked and belittled each other and ignored the needs of those with less power. By trying to live as kingdom people in the midst of the struggle, we hope not only to create healthier businesses, but also to change the very culture of our city. We must be able to see all people as created in the image of God whether they are poor and powerless, or rich and oppressive.

As we try to love our poor brothers and sisters, we will quickly discover that there is another worldly kingdom in opposition to the kingdom of God; one in which people are deeply invested, one they will defend with their lives. If we seek to look out for the interests of oppressed people, we must be willing to confront these systems, which are built on a love of money and power. Doing so may cause the wrath of these systems to fall on us like it did Jesus. Such is the price of seeking justice in the world. Like *Mammon*, these systems are spiritual powers, and they must be confronted not only by action, but also by prayer. These are big battles, but we can be confident his kingdom is surely coming, and that no power in heaven, on earth, or under the earth can stop it.

7

THE GREAT ROLE REVERSAL

There was a rich man who was dressed in purple and fine linen and who feasted sumptuously every day. And at his gate lay a poor man named Lazarus, covered with sores, who longed to satisfy his hunger with what fell from the rich man's table; even the dogs would come and lick his sores. The poor man died and was carried away by the angels to be with Abraham. The rich man also died and was buried. In Hades, where he was being tormented, he looked up and saw Abraham far away with Lazarus by his side. He called out, "Father Abraham, have mercy on me, and send Lazarus to dip the tip of his finger in water and cool my tongue; for I am in agony in these flames." But Abraham said, "Child, remember that during your lifetime you received your good things, and Lazarus in like manner evil things; but now he is comforted here, and you are in agony. Besides all this, between you and us a great chasm has been fixed, so that those who might want to pass from

*here to you cannot do so, and no one can cross from
there to us."*

—*Luke 16:19-26*

HAVING CONFRONTED THE PHARISEES ABOUT THEIR SELF-JUSTI-
fication in the face of the coming kingdom, Jesus gives
them a "wake-up call" parable regarding their wealth. The
parable of the shrewd manager, told to the disciples, was
meant to encourage his followers to be generous with their
earthly wealth, especially toward the poor, so that they
might have true, eternal riches. The emphasis is really on
the blessings of generosity with some teaching on the du-
plicity and power of *Mammon.* The parable quoted here is
clearly a warning of the dangers that lay ahead for those
who do not deal with these issues in their earthly lives.

This parable is a study in contrasts. There are two men
with radically different lives who end up in even more radically different places. Jesus begins by describing the life of
the rich man. The man dressed extravagantly in purple and
linen, which were expensive, imported items—the Gucci
and Armani of the time, the color of royalty.[1] The rich man
loved what was fine and desired to show his good taste
and wealth by what he wore. The color purple would not
have been more comfortable or kept you warmer; it was
an unnecessary luxury. His dress showcased his wealth
just as today's clothing does. Furthermore, the Greek
used here implies that this was his regular custom, not an
exception.[2]

Another thing we know about the rich man is that he ate sumptuously every day. The word for "feasted" is the same word used in the parable of the lost son when the father declared that they must *celebrate* since his son had been found. In other words, every day was a luxurious party for the rich man. Every day was a special occasion. It is interesting that Jesus chose to mention these two aspects of the rich man's lifestyle. Both food and clothing are necessary items; they are not luxuries we can do without. They can be purely functional, or they can be appropriately extravagant for the sake of celebration. The rich man's problem was that he made the extravagant his daily lifestyle. This was his first error.

Next, Jesus introduces us to the poor man. One of the first things we learn about him is that he has a name, Lazarus. In all of Jesus' teachings recorded in the four gospels, this is the only instance where a character in a parable has a name. That fact has led theologians throughout history to give different names to the rich man, but that misses the point. There is a reason that Jesus chose to name the poor man and not the rich one—the name Lazarus means "God helps."[3] As Jesus continues to describe the life of Lazarus, it seems that he has been misnamed. But Jesus' point here is that despite the appearance of Lazarus' earthly life, God has in no way forgotten him. Though the world has turned its back on him, he is not nameless or faceless to the creator of the universe, and in eternity God is his ultimate help. Even if Luke's readers didn't know the etymology of Lazarus' name, it is still clear that Jesus is emphasizing that he is a known person.[4] It is the rich man who remains unknown despite his worldly importance.

Lazarus lay at the rich man's gate. Likely, he was laid at that spot by someone else in order to beg, too weak to get there himself or remove himself to some other shelter.[5] Jesus goes into his physical torment in some detail: Lazarus was covered with oozing sores, he suffered from a lack of medical attention which must have caused pain as well as disgust from those who looked upon him, and he was so hungry that he would gladly have eaten anything that fell from the rich man's table. This is probably a reference to the bread that people would use instead of napkins to wipe their hands and then throw to the floor.[6] This bread was not suitable for any human to eat—it was waste, not leftovers—but he could not even get his hands on that. The description reminds us of the younger son's hunger and desire to feed on pig food.

In his weakness, Lazarus was unable to fend off the dogs that came to lick his sores. These were not your pet Golden Retrievers or Cocker Spaniels; dogs were dirty animals to the Jews, not pets. Many poor communities have problems with dogs multiplying and forming packs; they are left to fend for themselves and thus become some of the nastiest looking, inbred animals imaginable. I once saw a dog in Manila that looked like some hairless, demonic incarnation of a teddy bear. I would imagine that this was the kind of dog that added to Lazarus' suffering. In addition to indignity, contact with them would have made Lazarus unclean and unable to be in contact with other people.[7]

It was in this condition that Lazarus lay at the rich man's gate. The rich man had to pass by him every day. He noticed him and knew his suffering. In the afterlife—verse 24—the rich man asked Abraham to send Lazarus to dip his finger in some water to alleviate his suffering, which indicates that he recognized him and even knew his name. Lazarus was not unknown to the rich man. Yet despite his great resources, the rich man did nothing to help Lazarus. He saw Lazarus as neither a needy neighbor nor a lost brother; this was his second error.

One of the only things the two men have in common is that they both die; however, that common ground is lost quickly. Lazarus was carried away by angels to Abraham's side. The language might even mean Abraham's "lap," as if he were a child seated in the lap of his father.[8] The rich man, however, was buried (extravagantly perhaps) and finds himself in Hades.[9] There might be an implication here that Lazarus was not even given a decent burial—a final indignity.[10] The way these two men were treated in life—and then buried—were vastly different, but their eternal lives are completely reversed: the rich man's torment is contrasted with Lazarus' comfort in their common father's embrace.

Though the rich man once looked down on Lazarus, now he must look up to see him.[11] Lazarus had been lifted over him. Just as Lazarus would have taken any waste from the rich man's table, the rich man now wanted just a drop of water from Lazarus' diseased finger to cool his tongue. He appealed to his familial connection with his father Abraham. He did not address Lazarus directly, but asked Abraham to send him, indicating that he still viewed Lazarus as a lesser being meant to serve his desires.[12] Even in his torment he never repented; all he wanted was a break from his suffering.

Abraham's response to the rich man's cries might make us uncomfortable. He acknowledged that the rich man was in fact his child (verse 25), but that connection did not automatically gain him entrance into eternal peace, or even a momentary break in his torment. He had his good things and now he was justly suffering, whereas Lazarus had his suffering and now he was justly comforted. At first glance, it seems like Jesus is saying that good things in this life automatically guarantee suffering in the next and vice versa, but the message is more nuanced than this.

This is not the first time that Jesus has said something like this in Luke. In chapter 6, Luke records Jesus' proclamation of a series of blessings and woes:

> Blessed are you who are poor, for yours is the kingdom of God. Blessed are you who are hungry now, for you will be filled. Blessed are you who weep now, for you will laugh. . . . But woe to you who are rich, for you have received your consolation. Woe to you who are full now, for you will be hungry. Woe to you who are laughing now, for you will mourn and weep. (Luke 6:20-21, 24-25)

Jesus said that there would be a great reversal. Those who suffered, who were outcast and deprived, would find comfort and abundance, while those who sought wealth and comfort would find that the joys they pursued on earth were the only pleasures they would ever have. It fits within his larger teaching that those who seek to save their lives end up losing them, while those who lose their lives save them. The kingdom is good news for the poor, the needy, and the hurting, but it is a stumbling block for those who seek to gain the world. The values of the world are reversed in the kingdom of God.

But the rich will not become poor and the poor will not become rich simply because of their earthly experience. Within the context of the first parable in chapter 16 we understand that the reason the rich man ends up in torment is not because he was rich, but because he did not use his wealth to make friends with Lazarus, and so the poor man could not welcome him into the eternal homes. His sins were two-fold. First, he indulged himself with his wealth as a regular practice. While the parable does not go into this, we can infer from earlier teachings that he had an unhealthy relationship with his wealth and, therefore, God. The second sin was ignoring the plight of the poor man at his gate. He did not love his neighbor as himself. William Barclay wrote that the rich man "thought it perfectly natural and inevitable that Lazarus should lie in pain and hunger while he wallowed in luxury. . . . The sin of [the rich man] was that he could look on the world's suffering and need, and feel no answering sword of grief and pity pierce his heart; he looked at a fellow man, hungry and in pain, and did nothing about it."[13] We often think of sin as wrongdoing, but here sin is having the power to act and yet doing nothing.

His behavior contrasts that of the Good Samaritan as well as the father in the prodigal parable. These two men saw someone in need and suffering and responded with compassion immediately; they cared nothing for themselves, but sought to minister to the needs of the broken. Whereas here, the rich man sees Lazarus every day but never feels any compassion for him.

By not helping Lazarus, the rich man condemned him to a life of humiliation and suffering; the judgment that fell on him, therefore, is of the same kind. He gave no compassion, so he received none; he showed no mercy, so he was shown none. But the rich man's judgment was even more severe because of its permanence. Abraham not only responded that the rich man did not deserve any mercy, but also that neither he nor Lazarus could be merciful even if they wanted to. Lazarus in his goodness might have had compassion on the rich man and Abraham might have felt pity for his misguided son, but God took that decision from them.

The great chasm between true comfort and true agony, eternal wealth and eternal poverty, cannot be crossed. There is no more time for repentance. There is no more room for mercy. It is frightening and sobering, and we have to believe that Jesus intends for it to have that effect on us. Those of us who are wealthy and comfortable, and who ignore the suffering of the poor around us, are in jeopardy. Jesus is extending mercy to us now, but if we fail to repent and live generously we could end up on the wrong side of the Grand Canyon with no way back. Some that are lost are never found. It is an issue of life and death.

Over the next few chapters, we will look at the life of Lazarus and how the rich man should have responded to him. But for the remainder of this chapter I want to look at the rich man's first sin—self-indulgence. I have touched on this a bit already, but it is a sickness in our culture that I fear the church does not address regularly and, therefore, deserves a good bit of time.

The rich man's sin was not simply that he valued good things or extravagance, but that he made them center-pieces of his lifestyle. It is not wrong for us to be extravagant periodically, but it should be the exception not the norm. In my experience, the more you engage in something, the less special it becomes, and you therefore have a greater desire for something even more luxurious. The more we eat out, the less special it becomes. The more clothes we buy, the more shopping we have to do before achieving that celebratory feeling. Like a drug you need larger and larger doses of to get back to that first high, self-indulgence dulls our appreciation of the special.

I doubt that any of us think we are being indulgent in our lifestyles; our extravagances have become common to us. Even multi-millionaire athletes and executives believe that their salaries are merely providing for their families. No matter how much we have, we all think we are just getting by because we create lifestyles that fit, or sometimes even exceed, our incomes.

I expect that many of you, especially those with kids,

saw the movie *Wall-e*. It was a great critique of consumerism and its potential destructiveness. In the movie, consumption gets so out of control that the planet becomes one giant trash heap and needs to be abandoned. On their luxury spaceship, the people become so self-indulgent with food, technology, and leisure that they forget how to walk. They become unable to see any world beyond their personal video screens. When I was growing up, the great collective fear was that we would all die in a nuclear holocaust; now the fear is that we will drown in our self-indulgence. I think the latter is more likely.

One of the ways to shake us out of our numbness is to have contact with the poor at the gate. I never realized how rich I was until I knew how poor other people were. I did not realize how extravagant some of my lifestyle was until I saw how many people had trouble just getting enough food for the day. One of the church leaders in a Manila community told me how she often just drank coffee for meals when they could not afford to cook more than one meal a day. I have neighbors who crowd six adults and three children into a two-bedroom, 750-square foot house. This is one of the reasons that God says the rich need to be in relationship with the poor: when we distance ourselves from the poor, we become blind to our own wealth. If we only interact with middle-class Americans, we can deceive ourselves into believing that most of the world lives that way. Objectively, we know this is not true; it is a self-deception of convenience.

Having lived in a poorer community for over sixteen

years now, I sometimes feel a heightened sense of awareness when I visit a more affluent community. I am conscious of the luxury cars, expensive clothing, and pricey
restaurants. It is a discomfort I am glad for because it
means I have not become accustomed to such things. I
do not despise these luxuries or the people who indulge
in them. I simply recognize that they are luxuries and not
necessities. Some may question our decision to raise our
daughter in a struggling community where violence is
prevalent. They may believe that we are subjecting her to
unnecessary dangers and not providing her with the best
chance to succeed in life, but I believe that it would be a far
greater danger to raise her surrounded by affluence. The
influence of wealth may be helpful in creating successful
people in the world, but not kingdom-minded people.

I once spoke with a woman who had been involved with
a ministry to college students for much of her life. She told
a story about when her family was young and struggling to
make it on their missionary support. At this point in time,
the family often received groceries from friends so they
could have food for the week. One day, one of their children went to play at a friend's house. The friend's family
was considerably better off. When the daughter asked her
friend's family where they got their food from, they told her
that they got it from the grocery store. When she returned
home, she asked her mother how her friend could know
God's provision if her family was able to buy everything
they needed without any help. We may believe that we are
loving our children by providing for them extravagantly, but
we may in fact be denying them important spiritual lessons

and establishing lifestyle expectations that could affect their relationships with God.

It is not easy to make lifestyle changes voluntarily. It requires a fair amount of reflection and some resolve. Such changes usually come one intentional step at a time, not all at once. Let me present a few questions to get us thinking about what specific changes we may need to make.

Is Our Generosity Limited Because of Our Lifestyles?

Those of us who grew up in the church often believe that, somewhere in the Hebrew Bible, God instituted a tithe of ten percent of our incomes to be used to support his ministry. In fact, if you go back and read the texts that deal with tithing, you will discover that there were a number of purposes for the tithe, including supporting the ministry (Num 18:21), funding your own celebration (Deut 12:17), and providing for the needy (Deut 14:28-29). The idea of giving ten percent to ministry is a model many churches encourage their congregations to follow, despite the fact that only about five percent of Christians give that much or more.[14] I have to add that the idea of tithing is not really that present in the New Testament: Jesus' teaching, as we have seen, is that we should not limit our giving to a certain percentage, but that we should give as much as we can to those who need it. Faithful stewardship of our wealth means using it to bless others without arbitrary limits. It is that kind of sacrificial giving the kingdom seeks, but most of us do not even do what the Law requires.

Twenty-first century Americans are some of the wealthiest people in history, but we are unable to be significantly generous with our wealth because we determine our lifestyles by our incomes. We set our lifestyle first, and then give what we have left over. First, we buy the house, the car, and the clothing, and then we give what we can out of what we have left. Should it not be the other way around? We should determine how much we want to give first and then base our consumption on what is left. If we cannot even give ten percent of our incomes, then most likely we have a lifestyle problem.

I also need to say a little about accumulating debt. I write this out of my own convictions as we have fallen into debt in the last couple of years and are working now toward freedom from it. Our society runs on credit: there are some transactions that require a credit card, and banks depend on our indebtedness. Credit cards are one of the most convenient and destructive forces in our society because they allow us to believe that we can afford more than we actually can, and banks continually find ways to increase the interest rates and fees on the money we borrow so it becomes difficult to get out of debt once in it. It is legalized usury and most of us voluntarily enter it to maintain our lifestyles. If credit is a way we feed a lifestyle we cannot really afford, then we need to think about cutting up our cards.

What Should We Get Rid Of?

The first step in adjusting our lifestyles is reflecting on what we actually need and what luxuries we could do without. In doing such reflection, we will likely come up with some unnecessary luxuries we need to get rid of because they have an adverse effect on us spiritually. I would suggest that if there is anything that we are horribly afraid of losing or unwilling to let others use, we should think seriously about giving it away. If there is anything we believe we cannot live without, then we have to ask ourselves what power over our happiness we are giving this object. If we have things that we own to make us feel better about ourselves—or better than other people—then we need to consider liberating ourselves from them.

Our possessions can often own us. We are not all called to give everything away, but we do all need to consider giving away those things to which we have too much attachment. Over the years, my family and our neighbors have been robbed on occasion. At first, and oddly to me, several of my neighbors would respond to being robbed in a similar manner: "They must have needed it more than we did," they would say. That was never my feeling; I felt violated and angry. I assumed the robbers were greedy and disrespectful toward me because they were willing to take what was mine. But those who are poorer sometimes have an easier time sympathizing with the desperation that leads one to steal. My neighbors did not think it was good to be robbed or that the robbers were in some way noble, but they knew that possessions have a tendency to come and go, which is a healthy attitude. Our possessions are meant to serve us and be a means of blessing others. If we are serving our possessions and protecting them from others, then they need to go.

What Do We Really Need?

I watched a television program a while ago that featured a family of people who called themselves "Freegans." They believed that they should live on what other people threw away. They finished off the food people left on their plates and made arrangements with restaurants to take things they were going to throw out. They also dumpster dived, finding quite a bit of decent food that stores chose to get rid of. I am not sure I would advocate the "Freegan" lifestyle, but it teaches us that it is possible to live off what most Americans throw away. We consume so much that even our discarded food could sustain people.

The first step then is to curb the desire for things we really do not need: things we buy and never use, things that get stuck in a closet somewhere and are forgotten—these are more obviously unnecessary. Then there are those things we do use, but do not really need—this requires a little more reflection. These may be items or services we could live without: we may not need to eat out or own a second car or take an expensive vacation. We may not need to go out to the movies or install cable, a DVR, or even a television, let alone several, in our homes. Then there are those things we may in fact need, or at least feel peace from God about having, but of which we can have simpler and less expensive versions. We may feel it is right that we own a home, but it does not have to be the best house we can afford. The same would be true of cars, clothes, home furnishings, electronics, and food. The rich man's sin was that he made the functional, extravagant. We should be content with the functionality of our possessions and not worry about fineness or whether they are communicating something about our own worth.

We can also save money by purchasing things used. There is no reason that all our possessions have to be new. It is far less wasteful to reuse items that others no longer need. I am a big fan of Craigslist. I have purchased two cars off the website and furnished our living room and Servant Partners' office entirely with used items. Years ago when my wife sent out invitations to her baby shower, she said that she welcomed used items as gifts. Our poorer friends were able to give from things they already had and others loved the idea of scavenging for cool items in thrift stores. Buying used can save us some money; however, it is the big-ticket items that have the potential to free up the most financial space. We can save a lot on housing by renting in a less expensive area or buying a cheaper house than we qualify for. Our tendency, though, is to buy the nicest house we can afford, or even one just out of reach; one of the elements of the financial crisis was that people bought houses they could not really afford. If we reflect on what we really need in housing, we might find that we could have hundreds, and potentially thousands, of extra dollars a month. It might require living in a less nice neighborhood or having less space, but it could translate into huge savings. The same is true for cars and technology.

The last area I will mention is what I call the "nickel and dime" category. Many of us spend a good deal of money three to ten dollars at a time. We get a coffee, go out to lunch, buy some small piece of jewelry, or purchase a new plant for the patio. By themselves these items seem cheap, but they add up over a month. It is probably a good practice to analyze your monthly spending every once in a while to see where your money is going. You might be surprised.

We could also simplify by learning to recreate without owning. Most everything costs money—soccer clubs, ballet classes, music lessons—but there are many free or low cost things that we can take advantage of, like libraries, parks, and city programs. Our culture has become more aware of how much energy we consume, which is great, but we have to become aware of our other forms of consumption. Just because we can afford it, does not mean that we should buy it.

How Can We Simplify by Thinking More Communally?

One of the distinctive marks of the early church was that they held everything in common. We could cut back on our spending a great deal if we followed their model by giving away what we do not need and lending the things we have. In our church community, we have the practice of sharing our possessions. For example, when a child grows out of some piece of clothing, rather than being put away for a future child, it gets passed on to someone else in the church or the neighborhood. The same is true of toys and baby supplies. Because of this, my wife and I have had to spend very little money on kids' stuff. Similarly, there was a long phase when we had very unreliable vehicles, and generous friends would switch cars with us when we needed to do longer road trips to visit family. I now own a truck in part so that people can borrow it when they need to move things. My neighbor and I share yard equipment. A couple of the families in our church have weekly potluck dinners for whoever wants to show up and bring whatever they can. We are probably not unique; I am sure there are some neighborhoods and churches that work this way. What if we consciously decided that we would make what we have available to others so that they did not have to buy it? And what if, when we thought of purchasing an item, we asked ourselves if it is something we could borrow instead of buying and, if not, if it is something that we could make available for others to use?

We can also make more intentional communal decisions about our living situations. About ten years ago, Dave and Lisa Drake decided to buy the house next to ours so that we could minister together in our neighborhood and build community with each other. We eat together once a week, have an open Bible study in their home every other week, and built a gate between our yard and theirs, something our realtor told us never to do, so that we could benefit from each other's space—they have more open grass and we have more shade and space to ride bikes. When we throw parties, we will often use both yards. We sometimes borrow their van if we need to transport more people than we are able to with our car. We have keys to each other's homes and garages. Neither of our houses is larger than 1,200 square feet, but communally we have access to as much as most middle-class families. As a by-product of all this, we have become extended family to each other.

Others in our church have made even stronger communal decisions to live together in one home and share life together. They benefit from sharing resources and responsibilities: single people who live with families benefit from being part of a larger family, and people who could never afford a house on their own get access to one by sharing with another family. Some have even decided to hold all of their money together so that any larger financial decision needed the blessing of the larger group. These are just some examples of how we can save money and control our lifestyles. If we start to put some effort into it, we can come up with some really creative ways to think more communally.

All this being said, we must be careful not to be legalistic in these areas. Jesus never says that the people who own BMWs are going to hell, while those who own Kias are going to heaven (though most Prius owners seem to think they are holier than everyone else). The important thing is that we examine our hearts and honestly reflect on our lifestyles and possessions. We must lay them all on the altar before God and ask him what we need to give up so that we will not be tempted to worship them over him. Different people, then, will need to give up different things. What causes one to sin may not affect another; there is no universal definition of a simple life. It is a life-long struggle that has different challenges as one passes through different life phases. But the goals are always the same: to eliminate the objects or ways of life that we look to for joy and security instead of God, and to free up room in our lifestyles to be sacrificially generous. It would be an indictment upon us if we were unable to feed the starving because we felt a need to eat out more often.

In 1979, the Presbyterian Church of the United States made a statement about the need to simplify our lives:

> We believe Christ calls us to dissent from our present lifestyles and to make a radical break from the patterns of over-indulgence, consumerism and reckless waste. We are called individually and ecclesiastically to choose a lifestyle which more nearly reflects the simplicity of Jesus' life and allows us to identify with the poor and powerless throughout the earth. Such an altered lifestyle enables us to reconsider what we truly value in life, how we measure success, where we live, what we eat, how we use energy, how we invest our lives and resources, and where and how we travel. In short, we are challenged to live more simply that all may simply live.[15]

Would it not be great if all American Christians understood this as part of living out the kingdom? One of the things I have come to realize is that it is very difficult to change one's lifestyle apart from a community that shares the value for simplicity. As we noted earlier, we often determine our lifestyles by those with whom we associate. Over the years, I have observed that those who continually mark their lives by simplicity and generosity surround themselves with people who have the same convictions. Where your community is, there your heart will be also.

In his teaching, Jesus is not commanding us all to become ascetics, although there may be people who choose that life for personal and prophetic reasons. The rich man's sin was not that he indulged himself at all, but that it became routine for him—and at Lazarus' expense. Similarly, we do not have to give up everything that gives us pleasure, but we must resist the temptation to make luxury our lifestyle. Failing to reflect regularly upon our lifestyles puts us in danger of following in the footsteps of the rich man in this parable. Conviction and declarations are great, but we need to move toward real change in our lives.

8

AT THE GATE AND BEYOND

And at his gate lay a poor man named Lazarus,
covered with sores, who longed to satisfy his hun-
ger with what fell from the rich man's table; even the
dogs would come and lick his sores.

—*Luke 16:20-21*

FOR A FEW MONTHS, OUR FAMILY LIVED IN TAXCO, MEXICO. Every day, I would pass people who beg, and the town was small enough that I began to recognize these people. There was the older woman who asked for money in front of the Oxxo store—a Mexican equivalent of 7-11—the blind man who played an old guitar with only four strings on my way to the bank, and the man with one leg who asked for handouts in the market place. The poor and the rich live closely there. For example, we lived in a comfortable, one-bedroom apartment just a short walk from the main plaza—prime real estate. The owner of our apartment complex lived next door in a large, three-story, Spanish colonial house, but on the other side of the complex was a tiny, dilapidated, cinderblock shack that had been there for many decades.

On my three minute walk down to the plaza, I passed several large houses, including the former home of William Spratling, the American professor who brought silversmithing to this colonial mining town, setting the stage for its modern transformation into the capital of Mexican silver. But amidst the large, comfortable homes was a house that had been subdivided into numerous run-down apartments. Many of the local indigenous population lived here just above squalor. They sold their crafts in the plaza from early in the morning until late at night when they finally gave up on the last tourist. I often had long conversations with one of the Nahua women, Gloria. The Nahua are the descendants of the ancient Aztecs and, at about two million people, are still the largest indigenous group in Mexico, but nearly five hundred years later they are still treated as second-class citizens. I once asked her to teach me how to say, "How are you?" in her native language, Nahuatl. She assured me it was easy, but then articulated some four-syllable word filled with soft "T's" and swallowed "L's." I just stared at her and said, *"Mande?"* ("Pardon?") She laughed.

When we were in Mexico, we were welcomed into the homes of the upper middle-class as well as the poorer working class, all of whom live within sight of each other. I must confess that it was somewhat disconcerting to walk past squalor on the way to my apartment. I wished I did not have to see it. In my life, I have become comfortable in the homes of the wealthy as well as the poor, but there was some discomfort in being exposed to both in the same place, to have neighbors who were both very rich and very poor. It made me more conscious of both groups' lifestyles as well as my own. Though I am not glad for the poverty that people suffer there, I am glad that it is not hidden from the rich as it often is in the United States. In the United States, we would have moved the poor away from such a touristy area and built boutique hotels to replace their homes. The rich do not want to have the poor bringing down their property values; we do not want the discomfort of having to know that someone lives radically differently than we do only a few blocks away. We do not want to buy luxury items in the sight of those struggling to survive.

The rich man passed by Lazarus every day. He ignored the poor man, but was not ignorant of him; he saw his suffering and knew his name. In Jesus' time, the rich and the poor seemed to have lived in close proximity similar to what I witnessed in Taxco. The sick and needy were always showing up with rich people around, sometimes even in their homes. It was not difficult to identify the poor person at the gate in his time; the poor are harder to find in the United States as we have moved our front gate out so far that we never have to see a person in need if we do not want to look. We may encounter them at the end of the freeway exit ramp, but we know that if we do not make eye contact they will go away. We never have to actually know them; we do not consider them our neighbors. The added challenge for Americans is that we must go out to the gate to be able to see those who are suffering there.

Who are the poor at our gate? I could give a bunch of statistics about poverty that might help us understand *what* the poor are, but statistics do not really help us understand *who* the poor are. They are not one cohesive group. They are infinitely varied. Let me tell you a few stories of people I have known and the groups they represent.

Bertha

Bertha was an elderly woman in our church. She was a little slow mentally, but she loved to be helpful. She came to the church office every day and stuffed envelopes or did whatever else needed to be done. She worked in the kitchen every week for the Meals on Wheels program, which feeds those who cannot get out of their homes. One Sunday my wife, Lisa, noticed that she was having trouble reading the church bulletin. She was beginning to develop cataracts and, to my wife's surprise, she had no primary doctor despite her age. My wife was able to get her to see an ophthalmologist who recommended surgery. As Lisa helped Bertha with her medical history, her life story began to emerge.

She was an orphan and had been placed in a mental hospital because there was no other public institution in which to place her in the early part of the twentieth century. There she slaved away for the State of California, cleaning the hospital with no remuneration or schooling until she was thirty. A Christian nurse befriended her and gave her a basic education, something the hospital thought unnecessary. When the nurse left the hospital, she gave Bertha her number and told her to call her if she ever needed anything. Upon turning thirty, Bertha decided that she had been used enough and left the mental hospital. The people there tried to discourage her, telling her that she had no hope of making it on her own. She called her nurse friend who took her in and helped her get on her feet with assistance from the state. She referred to that event as when she got her freedom.

As my wife was taking down her medical history, Bertha told her that the only surgery she ever had was a hysterectomy at the age of thirteen. When my wife asked why she had had that surgery, all she said was that they told her she was a "bleeder." My wife wondered if there had been a real medical need or if the state had simply made a decision to sterilize Bertha when she reached puberty. There was a good reason for this suspicion. Between 1909 and 1963 the State of California forcibly sterilized twenty thousand people it deemed "feeble-minded" or "defective."[1]

After her eye surgery, Bertha needed help with eye drops. My wife spent the first night with her and realized that she was living in squalor. Her unwashed clothes lay piled in her bedroom closet, her refrigerator was empty, and roaches had taken over the kitchen. From that point on, people in our church visited her regularly. They cleaned for her once a week, did her laundry, and bought her food that she would actually eat. Any healthy thing purchased went uneaten, so the goal became getting any calories one could into her. When her refrigerator died, the church bought her a new one. She had suffered much, but at the end of her life she was surrounded by love, by the only family she had ever known—the church.

God repeatedly commanded the people of Israel to care for the widow and the orphan. Their circumstances made them vulnerable, as they had no one to provide for them and no one to protect them from oppression. Since they had no family, they became everyone's responsibility. James reaffirmed the centrality of this value in the New Testament as well when he wrote that religion that is pure and undefiled is, in part, caring for the orphans and widows in their distress (Jas 1:27). There are many poor people like Bertha right in our midst. They may attend our churches or our schools, suffering silently without our knowledge. So many people slip into poverty because they have no one in their lives committed to keep them from falling.

Mr. Willy

The first apartment Lisa and I moved into after we were married was on 9th Street in Pomona. It was a pretty diverse group of people: African Americans, Latinos, and a couple of Vietnamese families. We discovered early on that the Vietnamese family next door to us had lived in our apartment before we moved in, but for some reason had moved one door down. We would soon learn why. Our other neighbor was an African American man in his sixties who we all called Mr. Willy. He was technically disabled with diabetes, but at 6'3" and about 220 pounds, he was still a formidable presence. He had Section 8 housing, which meant that the government paid his rent; half the people in our complex were Section 8.

Mr. Willy was a dear man, kind and generally soft-spoken. The problem was that he had two drug-addicted daughters who routinely came by in the middle of the night to beg him for money. At around two o'clock in the morning, they would bang on his door, which sounded exactly like someone banging on our door, until he would get up and let them in, usually after a half hour or more. Then they would scream at each other so loudly that we could hear every word. They would demand money, and he would refuse. Eventually he would give in and things would calm down, though sometimes in his anger he would first respond violently. As I indicated earlier, he was not exactly a helpless old man. This happened several times a week for over a year. We were still new to the city and did not know how to handle the situation. We did not want to call the police on our neighbor and we did not want to confront him, as we were not sure if he himself was involved in any drug dealing. We lost a lot of sleep that year.

Eventually, we decided we had to do something not only for our own sanity but for Mr. Willy's as well. One day, I talked to him about the problem from his point of view.

I told him I was concerned for him and that this pattern had to stop. To my relief, he agreed that it needed to end but did not know what to do. He felt he could not call the police on his own daughters, so I suggested that the next time one of them came over and started yelling at him I would call the police. He agreed. The next time it happened I did call the police. They took his daughter out of the house and warned her that if it happened again they would arrest her. She stopped coming in the middle of the night after that. The other daughter, who, I was told, had a warrant out for her arrest, never came by again. After a year of enduring the chaos of Mr. Willy's life, we all finally had peace—including Mr. Willy. We learned our lesson: one out of control life can disrupt an entire neighborhood, and sometimes confrontation can bring peace.

There is a great deal of entrenched poverty in our inner cities and remote rural areas. Generations of people are stuck in patterns that keep them from escaping poverty's grasp. Sometimes poverty is the result of personal choices, and sometimes it is due to systems that do not help and sometimes injure. In a land of great wealth and extravagance, millions of people are homeless; hopelessness and resignation run rampant. We, one of the wealthiest nations on earth, have one of the greatest disparities between rich and poor of any developed nation. According to one recent study, among developed countries only Chile, Mexico, and Turkey have larger gaps between the classes than America.[2] We consider ourselves the land of opportunity, but opportunity is not evenly distributed; we are marching steadily toward a society split between the haves and the have nots.

Many people in our urban poor communities have given up hope that things can get better, and as a nation we do not help alleviate that feeling. We allow our inner cities to bear the brunt of society's ills: here is where you usually find strip clubs, porn shops, prostitution, drug dealing, and environmentally dangerous businesses. The poor are certainly not the only clientele for this activity, but such industries often end up in poor people's backyards. If your community is free of pollution, trash processing, and landfills, then some other community (likely poorer and non-white) is dealing with the detritus of your consumption. Dealing with such issues in their communities adds to a culture of despair and makes it harder for people to believe change is actually possible. On top of this, the poor rarely feel that the local government and police are their allies.

Despite the greater amount of crime in poorer communities, the poor tend to turn to the police less often, which is sometimes difficult for people from more affluent communities to understand. I know that it is hard to police a crime- and gang-ridden area, and I would like to give them the benefit of the doubt that they want to serve their communities well; however, I have also witnessed how the police treat people in poor communities. They are often condescending and authoritarian; they seem to assume you are guilty until proven innocent, and they are prone to use force that many residents feel is excessive.

I have a female friend who was working in a poor neighborhood in Chicago. One night, she was walking home and a man started following her. She flagged down a police car and was arrested for prostitution as a result. She was able to convince the police that she was not a prostitute after she brought them to her apartment to meet her mother and saw that she had been given an award for her community service. Instead of apologizing, they let her off with a warning. Almost everyone in poor neighborhoods has some story of a bad encounter with the police. Because of this, they feel they have no one to call upon, so they often try to protect themselves or take the law into their own hands. I have one neighbor whose children were being threatened by some people from our neighborhood who are known for their gang affiliation. Instead of calling the police, my neighbor just went over to their house with his gun and told them that if they continued to mess with his kids, he knew where they lived. They stopped harassing his children. This is often the way the law is enforced in my community.

For many years there was a group house for convicted sex offenders on parole down the street from us. These houses have private owners who receive guaranteed rent from the parole department. There is a fixed limit as to how many people can live in one house, but that is often disregarded. There had been as many as six sex offenders living down the street from us at one time—some child molesters and at least one convicted of rape.

People have a right to be rehabilitated and reintroduced into society, and as Christians we need to love even these people. What I do not understand is why does their rehabilitation always have to be in a poor neighborhood? In California, you can find where registered sex offenders live on the Internet. Our city of 150,000 people has 188 sex offenders living within our borders—almost entirely in poor neighborhoods. The more affluent city just to the north of us, with a population of 37,000, has just nine people registered as sex offenders. We are a little more than four times the size but we have more than twenty times the registered sex offenders. Why do the group-home owners not buy a house in their own middle-class neighborhoods and put people there? They do not do so because most middle-class communities would not allow six sex offenders to live in their neighborhood. Also, since the government only pays a fixed amount per parolee, the homeowner would not make as much profit if he or she had to buy a more expensive home. The group home in our neighborhood was closed down last year after the house mysteriously caught on fire. Thankfully no one was hurt, but the owner decided to sell the property rather than reopen it as a group home.

Some people are glad to help the poor as long as they can keep them—and the problems they associate with them—at the gate. Society's ills get dumped on the poor because it is cheaper and because the poor do not often have the power or will to resist it. They do not like it any more than the middle-class does, but they are accustomed to living with things they do not want in their neighborhoods. Not only do we ignore the poor at the gate, we often heap our societal problems upon them, and then blame them for the stench.

John

I first met John almost twenty years ago when he was working for our church. I knew he had been in prison, but only later did he confide in me that it was for raping a woman. He was divorced and in a custody battle with his wife for rights to see his children. We helped him normalize his relationship with her so that he could have some relationship with his kids, and after a while they started coming to church with him. John always lived on the edge financially. Occasionally, he would ask me if I needed any work done at our house in exchange for some money. He would ask for the money up front and promise to do the work later, though he rarely followed through. He took advantage of my friendship on numerous occasions, and I got involved pretty deeply in his life—we prayed together and had long conversations about life and spiritual matters. But there was always something out of control about his life; he kept sabotaging himself.

One day, John was gone. I do not remember exactly how long he was gone, but it was a number of weeks. Then he just showed up again one day with little explanation of his departure. This became a pattern. He got a pretty good job outside the church, and within a week or two he disappeared again, leaving not only the church, but also his new employment. When he finally returned, he confessed that he was a drug addict and that these departures were because of drug binges.

We wanted to help him, but he was bent on self-destruction. We began to confront him more on his behavior; he did not care for this and, in anger, he vanished again. The next time I saw him was in the Jack in the Box near our church where the homeless often hang out. Surprisingly, he was glad to see me. He told me that he was living on the street. He was missing a few teeth and had lost a lot of weight, but he said he was happy. He had stop using hard drugs but had continued to smoke marijuana. "God can't get upset with me for smoking a little pot from time to time, Derek," he said to me. I must admit, when he asked for my phone number I was a little scared to get back into the chaos and manipulation of his life, but I gave it to him anyway. He did call me a while later, leaving a message that he had gotten off the streets and into rehab. I was happy for him, but I was reluctant to call him back because I did not know how to be involved in his life in a healthy way.

There are many poor people who create or at least contribute to their own bad situations, like the younger son in the parable. There are plenty of people who want sympathy and charity, but not help out of their current lifestyles. A few years back, a homeless man came to our church looking for help. We committed to finding him housing, but he was unwilling to stay in anything we found for him. He did not want to get into a program that would help him get off the streets. What he wanted was money, not help, and he became angry when he realized we would not help him in that way.

Then there are those who are caught in addictions or lifestyles they cannot easily leave—drugs, alcohol, and prostitution. It may be difficult to feel mercy for people who seem to choose self-destructive paths, but they need Jesus' work in their lives more than anyone. The father in the parable did not love his younger son any less because he was foolish, and he did not believe his son should continue to suffer under his own mistakes. We, too, need to love these people, even when they are hard to love. However, we also need to realize that working with people with such struggles may require some expertise. Homelessness, prostitution, and addiction are complex issues, and people suffering under them often need a great deal of assistance to make real changes in their lives. Even the homeless in our country are not one monolithic group. Some are mentally ill, some are addicts, and some are families who have simply fallen on hard times. Working with different people requires different approaches, but that should not keep us from trying to love people with serious problems. We just need to realize that we may need assistance from those who have been successful working with certain groups if we really want to help.

Ingrid

I met Ingrid while working with college students as part of the InterVarsity Christian Fellowship college ministry. She had come from Guatemala as a child, and despite not knowing English when she arrived, she was able to excel in school and attend a prestigious private college. Her mother was a single parent who had moved to Los Angeles to find a well-paying job—at that time, a woman in Guatemala had few such opportunities. Ingrid says that she was unaware of their financial situation when she was young. Her mother always made sure the kids had something to eat, even if that meant that she went hungry at times. After two and a half years, she found stable work as domestic help to an affluent family and was able to send for Ingrid and her sister, along with an aunt and her two children, to join her. Ingrid's mother's employers actually coordinated the "coyotes"—people who specialize in moving others illegally across the border.

Ingrid came when she was eight years old. Because she did not know any English, she was required to repeat the grade she had finished the year before in Guatemala. It was shaming to her to be older than the other children, and she would often lie about her age. It took about two years for her to feel comfortable with English, though she will tell you that she still hates when her accent confuses people. They lived in a nice, all-white, predominantly Jewish community in an apartment owned by the father of her mother's employer. The trade-off was that Ingrid experienced intense prejudice when they went to the market or walked down the street. When they first arrived at the complex, some of the tenants made up stories about the two girls messing around in the mailroom in order to get them kicked out. Her mom's boss knew the girls and knew these stories were not true, but Ingrid became aware that there were people who did not like her because of her ethnicity. She went through a period where she did not speak Spanish outside her home for fear of what people might think about her.

Ingrid would say that she never thought of her family as

having financial problems; she just thought that they did not have a lot of extra money. She did not feel free to ask her mom for things she wanted, but she was aware that she got what she needed. They lived paycheck to paycheck and were never able to save any money. They did not have health insurance and only went to the doctor or dentist when there was an emergency. The car they drove was owned by her mother's employer. Looking back now, she realizes that they exploited her mom's situation. They loaned her the money for the "coyote," but took the payments out of her paycheck for years. For ten years, she worked until six p.m. six days a week, cooking, cleaning, and helping to raise their five children, barely providing for her own family. After ten years of frustration, she finally quit. Later, Ingrid said, God redeemed the relationship; her mother was considered part of the family and was invited to important family gatherings.

In 1987, when Ingrid was in high school, her family started the process of becoming legalized residents through Amnesty. It was a great deal of work since they could not afford a lawyer. There were demeaning medical exams and scary interviews with the INS. It was difficult, but it redeemed the fact that they had come to America without documents. She felt God's hand in it, affirming that she was meant to be here, that she was meant to have the opportunities this country offered her.

When she graduated from college, she felt she needed to be reconciled to the Latino minorities she protected herself from while growing up—the Mexican Americans. She had distanced herself from them because of the racism she saw toward them and their differences in language and culture. She decided to become a teacher and work in a poor Latino neighborhood in East L.A. "I wanted to provide a service for those who were disadvantaged, to help provide opportunities and a hope for a better future, in the same way that I was given an opportunity," she told me.

We often ignore poor immigrants that come to the country illegally. This is of course a complex and controversial issue in our country. Such migration is part of a larger dynamic; the world is rapidly urbanizing, and newcomers, most of whom are poor, often overwhelm large cities. There may be good arguments for regulating immigration in the United States, but I would point out that such restrictions have always had a dark side in American history. Soon after we became an independent nation, Congress passed the Naturalization Act of 1790, which limited citizenship access to free, white persons. The first, but not the last, race-based immigration act was in 1882—called the Chinese Exclusion Act. There was little effort to hide its intended purpose.

Historically, racism has played a significant role in our decisions to limit who can come into our country and who can become a citizen. We must be careful to examine our motivations for wanting to keep certain people out. Currently, it is common to demonize immigrants who came without permission, labeling them criminals and blaming them for many of the ills in our society; many, sadly, try to make life difficult for these immigrants in the hopes that they will return to their home countries.

Immigration officials know that almost half of the people who are here illegally entered the country legally: they came on student and tourist visas and stayed.[3] Why do they not draw as much ire as those who risk their lives to sneak across our southern border? Is it because those who come illegally are usually poor? We do not seem angry with the equal number of middle-class people who are illegal, which suggests to me that the issue for most people is not really obeying the law. We simply do not want more poor people, especially poor people who speak another language and have a different culture. We fear they are a threat to our way of life, that they will be a drain upon us. The poor, whether legal or undocumented, do require things from society, but they have the potential to be great assets to the larger whole because they generally desire to improve their circumstances. It may be true that the poor create some additional costs to the economy, but from events over recent years it is quite evident that the rich have much greater potential to devastate the economy than the poor do.

I know a lot of undocumented people, the vast majority of whom are hard-working people desperate to escape the poverty that mired them in their home country. Some, like Ingrid, were brought as young children and given no choice, and now they live as second-class citizens in the only country they have ever known. People pay extreme costs for the possibility of a better life. They pay thousands of dollars for smugglers to take them across the border, they risk dying in the desert, and they separate families, often sending fathers and older children to labor on behalf of the larger family. While I was living in Mexico, I had a friend whose father was separated from the family for eight years so that his children could have a chance at a better life. Once in the United States, immigrants are forced into a black market economy. They create false social security accounts that they will never draw upon, they are exploited by employers who work them long hours and pay them below minimum wage, and they drive illegally and without insurance because most states will not issue them driver's licenses. President Obama has recently taken action to help millions of these people come out of the shadows. Although his methodology has left him open to criticism, he has rightly recognized that the current situation is simply unsustainable.

Illegality is a universal problem with the needy. For example, the homeless in our country often break the law by sleeping where they are forbidden to do so. I visit squatters around the world who live on land that does not belong to them. They often steal electricity from power poles to light their houses, and dump their trash in rivers. People sell, buy, and build without the permission of the government simply because they cannot afford to obtain it. Often, the poor are given a choice between obeying the law and surviving; given such a choice, the decision is not hard to make. Most who risk their lives to come to the United States do not do so because they dream of being richer; they come because they want to survive. If any of our families were stuck in extreme poverty and a possible solution lay across an imaginary line in the sand, would we not do the same? If obeying the law means dying in poverty, then is the law just?

Enacting laws that keep people trapped in poverty without the tools to escape is shortsighted and I fear will do more harm to our economy and communities in the long term. Some people are literally trapped. If you think slavery is dead in America, you are gravely mistaken; it exists unseen. Many people are brought to America with the promise of freedom, only to be put to work for pennies a day or forced into the sex industry. They are warned that if they try to communicate with any Americans, US authorities will punish them for entering the country illegally. They are held captive by fear, unable to ask for help and doubtful help would be given even if they asked. According to a study done by Free the Slaves, ten thousand people are enslaved at any given point in the United States. They also claim that the federal government estimates that 14,500 to 17,500 people are trafficked to the United States every year.[4]

I realize that illegal immigration is controversial and that there are many positions on this topic in the church, but the fact that certain people come to the United States illegally does not absolve us of the responsibility to love them as neighbors in the eyes of God. The nation of Israel was routinely commanded by God to take care of the sojourner. God realized that this people group, like widows and orphans, was vulnerable to exploitation and neglect. The people of Israel were to care for the sojourner because they, too, had been exploited strangers in a foreign land at one point in time. Is that not similar to our own national history? Except for Native Americans, African Americans who were brought here against their will, and those of Mexican descent whose families have been here since parts of our country belonged to Mexico, we are all immigrants whose ancestors came looking for a better life.

One side of my family were Mennonites who may have come to escape religious persecution; the other side were Jews who came to escape the Tsar. Should we not have more mercy on those who are simply seeking to do the same thing our families did—escaping one life in pursuit of a better one? And from a spiritual point of view, all of us who are Gentiles were foreigners to the nation of Israel and the kingdom of God, yet we were brought in and made citizens of a country to which we did not belong by birth. Our spiritual history should make us more gracious toward the outsider. As a church, we must recognize that there is a massive population that is suffering at our doorstep. If we saw them as brothers and sisters, I doubt we would be so quick to want to send them back or limit their rights here. God is always attentive to the cries of the poor. If we take actions that increase the suffering of the destitute, can we be so sure that we are on the same side as God?

Reyna

Reyna grew up in a small town of three hundred families

about seven hours outside of Acapulco, Mexico. She grew up without running water or electricity. At that time, thirty years ago, there were no paved roads or cars, and the main means of transportation were donkeys and horses. As poor farmers, her family lived off the land, eating what they grew and raised. Since they were only able to grow what they needed to eat, they had very little potential for income.

There was little extra money for "luxuries." Reyna owned two dresses and no shoes. She spent her days working on the farm, and because there was no money for pencils and paper, she never attended school. Eventually, her father got work as a police officer in a nearby town. Like so many millions of people in the past fifty years, her family then made the move to the big city. They started in Mexico City, but relocated to the smaller town of Taxco. Money was hard to come by in the city, but at least there were opportunities: you could go to school and buy clothes and food. Reyna's youngest siblings were eventually able to attend college. Reyna herself went to adult school, where she learned the basics of reading and writing, though she still does not feel comfortable doing either.

She and her husband, Lorenzo, are bright and amazingly hospitable. Unfortunately, they are limited in what work they can find. She cleans houses, cooks, and washes clothes; he works in construction. Lorenzo works from eight a.m. to six p.m. five days a week, and from eight a.m. to one p.m. on Saturdays for the equivalent of $150 a month—and living expenses in Mexico are not that much cheaper than the United States. If he gets injured, like he did a couple years ago when he fell off a roof and hurt his back, he does not work—and he does not get paid. Their unmarried children still live at home to help with expenses. Reyna and Lorenzo have worked hard to give their kids a chance to improve their lives. A couple of them are in college now, and one is working in the United States illegally.

The rural poor account for most of the poverty in the world, although that percentage was considerably higher a few decades ago. Like Reyna's family, the rural poor are flooding into their countries' major cities. Some nations have tried to stem the tide of urban expansion, but with such little chance of improving one's life in the country, few are inclined to stay there. Almost half of the world lives on less than two dollars a day.[5] It is unimaginable that so many people survive on less than what a Starbucks Frappuccino costs.

The numbers do not get much better after the first three billion people: eighty percent of the world lives on less than ten dollars a day.[6] Those of us making more than ten dollars a day are in the minority—both in our earnings and in our consumption. In 2005, the wealthiest twenty percent of the world accounted for seventy-six percent of private consumption. In contrast, the poorest fifth accounted for a mere 1.5 percent.[7] The statistics are sobering, depressing, and overwhelming. Middle-class Americans often think of themselves as the majority, but if you are a family with two children making fifty thousand dollars a year, you are part of the top five percent richest people in the world. The

Occupy movement has done a good job pointing out the economic disparity in the United States, but on a global scale we are not the ninety-nine percent. Do you know how much income you need to make as an individual to get into the top one percent? Fifty-two thousand dollars. Check out the "How rich am I" calculator on Giving What We Can's website. It is very eye opening. Of course, the cost of living varies greatly around the world—fifty-two thousand dollars goes a lot further in Bangkok than in Los Angeles, let alone London—and this fact relativizes these figures some. Nonetheless, we in the middle-class should not be deluded into thinking that we are among the vast majority of low wage earners.

Middle-class Americans are among the richest people the world has ever known. Therefore, we need to be aware of our comfort so that we do not overlook the great suffering that is around us. My goal is not to make us feel guilty, but to think about what we can do differently to love our poor brothers and sisters throughout the world.

There are millions of poor in our own backyard in the United States, but that does not negate the need to look beyond our immediate gate for those in need. In Acts 11:28, the prophet Agabus, while in Antioch, predicted that a severe famine would hit the world. The believers in Antioch—a mixed group of Jews and Gentiles—decided that they would send money, according to their ability, to the believers living in Judea to help them through the crisis. Paul and Barnabas were commissioned with the responsibility of bringing the gift to Judea. In Galatians 2, Paul records that when he and Barnabas went up to Jerusalem, the only request the Judean apostles made was that he remember the poor, which Paul says he was very eager to do (Gal 2:10). They were not concerned that Paul would forget about the poor in general; they were asking him to continue to consider the needs of the poor in Judea as he preached the gospel throughout the Roman Empire.[9] Paul stayed true to his word: he took up a collection for the saints in Judea among his converts. This collection is mentioned several times in his letters. Some of Paul's most significant teaching on generosity concerns this specific effort.

The Gentile converts had no national, biological, or physical connection to the Jewish Christians in Judea; however, they understood, aided by Paul's instruction, that they were linked to them spiritually. Most of those who gave never met the poor they helped, but they considered them brothers and sisters whom they were obligated to help. Throughout this book I have argued, as I will continue to do, that the rich need to have real relationships with people from different classes. This does not mean, however, that we should not help those poor so far beyond our gate that we cannot know them.

Cora

Cora grew up in a squatter community near the train tracks in Manila as one of ten children. Both of her parents worked, but it was not enough to support her family; sometimes all they had to eat for an entire day was a bowl of rice porridge. The local creek served as their toilet. When she was nine years old, she was hit by the train and lost her memory for a month. From age nine to seventeen, Cora worked as a vender selling peanuts and mangos on the street and in beer houses. She had dreams of becoming a teacher, but the long hours required to sell her products forced her to drop out in her sophomore year of high school.

Because of the competition with other kids selling the same things, she would beg outside of restaurants for food or money. If people left food on their table, she would sneak past the guards, who were meant to keep her out, and put the leftover food in a plastic bag so she could eat it outside. If she got a lot of food, she would bring it back to her family. She would sometimes try to sell in more affluent areas, which was illegal. Once, she was arrested for this and put in juvenile jail for three days. She recalls how the boys on the floor below would shout to get the girls' attention. They would cut themselves and write, "I love you" in blood on the walls.

Sometimes she sold food in the local dance clubs. When she was about fourteen, the club owners began offering her jobs as a stripper. They told her that if she worked as a dancer, she would make lots of money and not be as tired. A friend of hers worked in one of the clubs and told her that there was an upstairs secret room where customers could be alone with the dancers. Some nights, her friend said, she would only dance, but if she wanted to earn big money she would have to have sex with the men, some of whom became regular customers. One night, she told Cora, she had sex with five different men. Her friend cautioned her not to start working as a stripper. "It is not worth it," she said. "You will never get out once you start."

Cora recalls that the greatest suffering her family endured was at the hands of the police. Instead of protecting the people, they abused and extorted them. Authorities were not to be trusted, but feared.

In 2008, the government destroyed the only community she had ever known to make way for a new train system. Cora watched as workers removed all of their belongings from their house and set them where their neighbors' house used to stand. The men then went to work on Cora's house with sledgehammers—a home I had spent time in myself when I visited her community. Within thirty minutes, her house was reduced to rubble, and she was forced to move to a new community outside the city and start her life over.

It is difficult to even conceive of the sea of international poor people beyond our gate—some cities have slums of more than a million people. The needs are overwhelmingly great, leaving us to wonder what we could possibly do to put a dent in the problem of international poverty. My friend in Ghana, Rev. Dr. Joseph Mante, is fond of saying, "You cannot help everyone, but you can help someone." We should not allow the sheer amount of need to paralyze us. There are people's circumstances that we can help change if we are committed to doing so. There are also larger efforts we can become a part of that can deal with larger scale needs, but I will address these later.

9

LAZARUS COMFORTED

But Abraham said, "Child, remember that during your lifetime you received your good things, and Lazarus in like manner evil things; but now he is comforted here, and you are in agony."

—*Luke 16:25*

LAZARUS HAD A MISERABLE LIFE, AND YET HE WAS NAMED "GOD helps." As I mentioned earlier, one possibility for Jesus' choice to name this sole character in his parables was that although he was not helped by any human, God was his ultimate help. Another possibility—though not mutually exclusive—is that his name gives some insight into his spiritual state. Perhaps Jesus was communicating that, despite his suffering, Lazarus knew God was his helper and continued to trust in him. His physical state might have led people to believe that he was unrighteous, that he was being punished for some sin, but his name suggests a different identity, one where he knew God and was known by him. God becomes his ultimate comfort, not simply because he was poor, but because in his poverty he trusted that God was his only help.

It is a stark contrast: the rich man suffers in agony and the poor man is at peace at Abraham's side. The fact that Jesus chose Abraham to be his source of comfort emphasizes that Lazarus was an important child in the family of Israel. In the end, he was more a son of Abraham than the rich man. God is the final comfort for the poor and the suffering; he has a special concern for them, he seeks them out especially, and he is preoccupied with their well-being because often no one else is. They are the lost that he leaves the ninety-nine in the wilderness to search for. As we saw in Luke 6, Jesus even called the poor, the hungry, the mournful, and the persecuted blessed because of what God would do for them. He claimed that his ministry brought good news to the poor (Luke 7:22). But how exactly is the gospel good news for the poor? There are three places in Scripture that help us answer this.

Rich in Christ

Years ago, a group of friends and I got to visit Aling Nena in Manila. I mentioned earlier how her life was transformed by Jesus as he healed her of her addictions and criminal activity and gave her hope. She was still poor. Her house was a bit nicer than I understood it had been twenty years earlier, but it was still more dilapidated than almost anything in the United States. She began to complain a little bit about her living situation. She needed more money to do some construction on the house in order to have long-term renters, which would, in turn, provide her with some more income. Filipinos are masters of indirect communication, so I am pretty sure that it was a subtle request that we Americans help fund her dream. The pastor's wife, who was with us, gave her a gentle correction, and she caught herself and countered that though she was still poor, she was now rich in Christ.

It was Paul who reminded the Corinthians that Jesus had been rich but became poor so that by his poverty they, too, could become rich (2 Cor 8:9). Previously they had been spiritually poor, but Christ's grace lavished upon them made them rich.[1] They had received a foretaste of the true riches which are only found in relationship with Jesus. God welcomes back those despised by the world and makes them his children, heirs to his estate, and this has a special significance to those whom the world considers nothing. They are children of God, equal in value to those who are educated, wealthy, and important in the world. To know that the creator of the universe cares about them and desires a relationship with them is no small matter. Some time ago, a woman named Yut came to faith in our ministry in Bangkok. She had tried to be a good Buddhist, but in Bangkok this required going to the temple often and "making merit," that is, offering money as sacrifices at the temple. Reflecting on her life, she could not see what benefit all those sacrifices had gained for her. Being poor and in debt with two children, she believed she could not afford to be a good Buddhist. When she decided to follow

Jesus, she said, "Even if I don't see God's miracles in my life, just knowing I'm his child, that I haven't been abandoned, that's enough."

Our Servant Partners worker, Sara Stephens, wrote me about Yut:

> Yut recently suffered a miscarriage and also had a fortune teller speak lies over her about dying by age thirty, both of which convinced her that she was full of bad karma. After praying as a group, and specifically the pastor praying to cut ties with those lies, she said she felt much more at peace and just looked visibly more joyful. It's such good news for the poor who are under the law of karma to know that they are pure and spotless to God—they've for so long believed their suffering and poverty were a just punishment. I think Yut received hope for the first time that her life could change, and that she's loved.

Since her conversion, Yut has struggled in her relationship with Jesus. This is not unusual among the urban poor; very often the healing that is necessary for people who have experienced so much pain and trauma takes time. But Jesus revealed himself to her and called her his child, and we know that he is able to protect the work he began in her.

While a true relationship with Jesus makes everyone rich, there are some ways in which the poor have a unique wealth compared to the rich. James argued that the poor should be treated equally well as the rich because, among other things, God has chosen them to be rich in faith as well as fellow heirs of the kingdom (Jas 2:5). It is true that the poor often have greater faith than the rich, which, in my experience, is because they have a much better sense of their need for God. When you have little money and little status in the world, to whom else can you turn? If you do not have health insurance, you learn to pray for healing. If you do not have money or savings or credit, you learn to pray that God will supply your daily bread. We who are not poor can be tempted to rely on our money or possessions for comfort. Wealth dulls faith.

Many of my poorer friends have incredible stories about ways in which God has answered their prayers. When things looked bleak, God came through for them time and time again. Often, their first impulse when met with a need is to pray. I usually begin with trying to solve the problem and pray after I have some potential options or when I realize I have no solution. While we cannot generalize to say that all poor Christians are more faithful than all rich Christians, as a rule they have a better understanding of what it means to trust God. It is a richness that some of us with more earthly resources are poor in.

The poor are rich in generosity and trust of God. Earlier I cited the story of the widow who gave two copper coins to the temple treasury, and Jesus made sure the disciples recognized that the poor widow had actually given more than all the other rich people because she had given everything. He was not concerned with the amount that was put in, but the sacrifice in the giving. We may give a great deal of money away, but if we give it out of what we can afford, it is less than those who give out of their poverty, even if the amount is smaller.

In the kingdom, generosity is not measured by monetary value, but by sacrifice. In an effort to encourage the Corinthian churches to give generously to the poor in Jerusalem, Paul told them that the Macedonian churches had given sacrificially to the collection, far more that they were asked even though they themselves were very poor (2 Cor 8:2). It has been our experience that it is difficult to out-give the poor. Once, when some friends and I visited a family in a squatter community, the mother sent her daughter out to buy sodas for each of us. The pastor who accompanied us remarked later that it probably cost them all the money they had. Many people have been generous to me in my life, but no one had ever given me everything they had in order to bless me.

The poor are rich in community. They often consider not only their own needs, but also those of their extended families and communities. This stems from practicality; the poor often have a sense that they are "in this together." They need each other to survive and are therefore more likely to help their needy neighbor or relative, realizing that someday they, too, will need help. Because of this, poor communities tend to be more interdependent.

There are some costs of such interdependence. In squatter communities, it is common for neighbors or family members to ask you for money if they perceive you have some excess, which makes saving difficult. People end up living day to day, unable to build the resources that would help them escape poverty. While this feeling of responsibility for the larger community is deeply biblical and should be encouraged, it is important to encourage individual fiscal responsibility as well.

The poor are rich in humility. They tend to care less about status and position in the world, whereas wealth, job titles, education, and positions in society give the wealthy reasons to be arrogant. Those without position in the world are more likely to model a Christ-like humility. They generally value servanthood as they do not think service is beneath them, and they do not expect to be waited upon. When the woman we hired to wash our clothes in Mexico came over to visit, she had a hard time not cleaning up the dishes or watering our plants. We had to forbid her from doing these things while she was a guest, but in her mind being a guest did not mean she did not need to serve. Service was in her character. Jesus modeled the life of a servant: he washed the feet of his followers because he was not above such concrete service. The rich are quickly tempted to think they are above such things.

The poor have a richness in Christ that the larger body of Christ needs. We need people of unusual faith, generosity, community, and humility to encourage us toward the fullness of Christ. I am not arguing some notion that all poor Christians are stronger than their rich brothers and sisters in these areas, nor am I arguing that it is good for people to be trapped in poverty because it can build faith, humility, etc. What I am arguing is that Jesus can redeem people's poverty in a way that develops these aspects of Christian character. James' caution for us is that we dare not look down on such people—their faith and character might well exceed our own.

Not only are the poor rich because of what Jesus has done for them, they are rich because of what he is doing in them now. Aling Nena's life was changed from one of addiction and crime to one of Christian leadership. Yut's life is being transformed from one of merit and resignation to one of grace and hope for the future. In the third century, Celsus, a pagan lawyer and critic of Christianity, derided Jesus as a flawed teacher, for, he argued, "While others cry, 'Come to me, you who are clean and worthy,' Jesus calls, 'Come to me, you who are down and beaten by life'; and so, being taken at his word by these impossible people, he is followed about by the rag tag and bobtailed of humanity trailing behind him."[2] The church father, Origen, responded to Celsus in his work *Contra Celsus*:

> *You say that poor Christians are the rag tag, and bobtail of humanity, but he does not leave them that way; but out of material you would have thrown away as useless, he fashions (men and women), giving them back their self-respect, enabling them to stand up on their feet and look God in the eyes. They were cowed, cringing, broken things. But the Son has made them free.*[3]

Jesus does not leave the poor broken; he promises to transform them. They may have been weak, given over to destructive vices, and insecure about their importance in the world, but he makes them strong and mature, full citizens and leaders of the kingdom of God.

The Kingdom of God Lived Out

Just because those who are poor are now rich in Christ does not mean that all their sufferings magically go away or that their poverty no longer bothers them, as was evident from Aling Nena's complaint about her living situation. Lazarus trusted in God, but he still suffered immeasurably in his life. How can a good God allow those he loves to continue to suffer like Lazarus? In the parable, it was clear that God expected the rich man to help Lazarus; the people of God are his answer to the evils of poverty.

The early church understood this. In Acts 2 and 4, Luke describes the life of the church in Jerusalem. He said that the people were in awe because of the signs and wonders being done in their midst. They spent time together in the temple and ate in each other's homes. But in both chapters, Luke emphasizes that one of the distinguishing marks of the early church was that they were generous to each other—and to the poor specifically. In Acts 2:44-45 and 4:32, we see that no one claimed ownership over any possessions, but rather shared them with everyone. In 4:34, we learn that there were no underprivileged people in their community because whenever there was a need, someone sold one of their possessions to meet it. For a while it seems the Acts community eliminated poverty. Newly filled with the Holy Spirit, they actually lived out what Jesus had commanded. They were faithful stewards of their wealth.

The fact that the early church demonstrated generosity to the needy immediately after they received the Holy Spirit, as well as the fact that Luke mentions it twice, seems to imply that they, and Luke, understood this to be a central manifestation of the kingdom in their midst. They considered Jesus' instruction about money and the poor as primary to what it meant to be a follower of Jesus, a natural outworking of Christian community. Most likely, this was directly related to the grace of the Holy Spirit in their lives: because God was so generous to them, they became naturally generous toward each other.

When Paul was encouraging the Corinthian churches to give to the collection for the poor in Jerusalem, he wrote:

> I do not mean that there should be relief for others and pressure on you, but it is a question of a fair balance between your present abundance and their need, so that their abundance may be for your need, in order that there may be a fair balance. As it is written, "The one who had much did not have too much, and the one who had little did not have too little." (2 Cor 8:13-15)

It is not our goal to make the poor rich—they do not need to become enslaved to *Mammon*—the goal for the kingdom is balance and interdependence. There should not be some living in self-indulgence while others die of hunger. Viv Grigg, who leads a master's program on urban poverty, has told me that, in his experience, when rich and poor believers come into relationship with each other things naturally tend to equalize. Acts demonstrates this. It is hard to ignore the needs of a poor brother or sister that you know.

The gospel is good news for the poor because the people of God are supposed to live out the values of the kingdom and share their resources with the needy. There were safeguards set up in the nation of Israel intended to care for the poor as well (as we will see later in the book), but Israel continually fell short just like the rich man in the parable. Where Israel failed, the kingdom is meant to succeed. There should be no needy person among us. The fact that there are so many poor in a country as rich—and supposedly Christian—as ours should tell us that something is wrong. But can we call a nation Christian that is so given over to consumption and avarice and, despite its wealth, has no consistent concern for the poor? The United States looks a lot more like the rich man than the early church, and that should greatly concern us.

But what should concern us even more is that the American church looks more like America than it does a people consecrated for God. The church at least should be a place where there is no poverty. Of course, there are a lot of churches without any poor people, but that is often because they were never there in the first place. The kingdom is God's solution to poverty in this fallen world. If we fail to live out his command to take care of each other, we play a role in robbing the poor of the good news of the gospel.

The Eternal Kingdom

Lazarus died in poverty, and he is not alone; tragically, thousands die every day in just the same way. Many are Christians with whom we, by the grace of God, will spend eternity. They will die unaided by their governments and the Christian church, but as was true with Lazarus, God has not forgotten them.

I have dabbled in art for many years and have at times tried to depict the look on Lazarus' face when he finally found his first moment of peace and joy, his first moment free of pain and torment.

Once when I was in Honduras, I came down with food poisoning—along with much of our group. That night was the longest night of my life. I was living by myself in a ten square foot cinderblock squatter house, where the only furniture was an old bed. The room was roach and mosquito infested. The more challenging part, though, was the common toilet in the courtyard shared with two other families. It was just a pit toilet with a cement "bowl" to sit on if you so desired. The roaches grew nice and big down below. The door to the toilet was comprised of several planks that *mostly* shielded your activities inside. Normally I did not mind these conditions, having lived for periods of time in such situations, but when I got sick it became hell.

Every fifteen minutes I had to get up to relieve myself. I could not even keep down water. At first, I loathed the idea of putting my face in a hole stinking of refuse while rodent-sized cockroaches climbed out. I was conscious of my neighbors hearing me retch or seeing me through the two-inch cracks in the door. But after hours without sleep and horrible discomfort, I no longer cared where my head was or what vermin crawled on me or who heard or saw my misery and nakedness. I just wanted it to end. There were a couple of times that I wished for death. That night seemed like an eternity, but morning eventually came and the dry heaves stopped. I started to get better. The relief was almost a spiritual experience. After being in such suffering, having it end was an indescribable joy.

Although it seemed like forever, that suffering was only one night. What must Lazarus' joy have been like after a lifetime of suffering? The good news of the gospel for those poor who trust in God is that no matter what they suffer in this life, no matter how little they are helped by anyone else, he will end their pain. He will be their comfort. He will be their rest and wealth. The poor will inherit the kingdom. They will feast at the great banquet.

God promises to comfort those who suffer; he also promises that the rich will face judgment. Abraham's words to the rich man are not only a warning for the wealthy, they are a blessing for the oppressed. The Hebrew Bible taught the poor to cry out to God for justice if the wealthy would not help them (Deut 15:9). In the story of the rich man and Lazarus, Jesus promises that God will be true to his word to bring justice. He will not fail to punish those people who do evil to the vulnerable. It is likely that Jesus' audience heard this parable with precisely this understanding.[4]

It might make us uncomfortable to think that God's punishment should be a comfort to anyone, as we tend to be fonder of the merciful side of God than we are with the just side. But it is in fact good news to know that he will not tolerate evil forever. Those who have suffered from injustice can know that there will come a day when things will be set right. They can know that those who have oppressed them—or even simply ignored them—will have to stand before God and answer for their actions (or lack thereof). Though they may be denied justice every day of their lives, they will find it in eternity with the judge of the universe.

Ema Smith's Story

It is one thing for me to say that the gospel is good news for the poor, but it is another to hear it from the poor themselves. Ema is one of our Servant Partners staff in Manila and grew up in a squatter community there. This is her story of finding Jesus amid destitution and how God ultimately called her to stay and minister among her fellow poor:

> We moved to a house near the squatter railroad community in Balic-Balic when I was five years old. It is stupid to build your home right next to an active railroad track, but when faced with no other options we moved there. Life on the tracks was difficult. Homes were built so close to the rails that the train

would sometimes scrape the roofs. Babies died from being hit by the train. One day, I returned home and saw a puddle of blood from a man who had been hit. Luckily he survived. Drug dealers openly sold their drugs (crystal methamphetamine), and addicts would take drugs in the open. Even young children could be seen sniffing rubber cement.

When I was young, I was not aware that we were poor. Eventually, I realized that we were poor because we did not have a bathroom and running water in our house. We had to fetch water from a community faucet, which was fifty yards away. And we had to use a pay community bathroom, which was even farther, about two hundred yards. I also remember thinking that most of our neighbors were rich. My cousins were rich because their father had a good job at that time. One of our neighbors was considered wealthy because she had two daughters that were working in Japan as "entertainers," meaning they were exotic dancers and/or prostitutes. They had expensive toys that all the kids envied. We had another neighbor who I considered rich because their children were studying in a private school. I used to like it when this neighbor invited me to their house to play and sometimes to eat. I remember when I was young my measurement for whether somebody was rich or poor was what ketchup they used. I used to think that the Del Monte tomato ketchup was what rich people ate. The poor used banana catsup. They had tomato ketchup, and I was happy to eat it when they invited me over.

Life was difficult for me when I was young. My father has never held a permanent job. He is an alcoholic, a gambler, and a smoker. Growing up, he spent more money on his addictions than on our needs. It was hard to go to school because he would steal our lunch money. He would sometimes drink with his friends in the house until late at night making it hard to do homework and sleep. My mom worked part time to support our family. She would cook breakfast food and sell it in front of our house in the morning. She also sold uncooked ramen noodles. My parents would often fight. The fact that my father did not have work did not keep him from drinking. He just ran up debt at a local store. This caused a lot of conflict between my parents.

Five of us lived in a house that was about twenty-five square feet. At one point, my grandfather also lived with us, and at another time also my aunt and her husband lived with us. Because my father did not work regularly, we would often eat just rice with water and salt, or rice with water and sugar if we had sugar. When we would get sick, we did not go to the doctor. We just hoped that the sickness would go away. I am thankful that I did not have a serious illness that required going to the hospital.

I became a Christian when I was eleven years old. In May of 1990, the year before I became a Christian, there was a big fire in our community. Since houses in our community were built almost on top of each other, even a small fire could cause a great deal of damage. Classes started in June, and my mother had already bought uniforms, shoes, and school supplies for us. Our home burned down, and we lost everything. We were renting and the owner did not have money to fix our house quickly, so we had to move in with my mother's relatives. They were a little bit better off, so they had space for us to sleep on their living room floor. That was really hard for us children. I am the oldest of three children. After a few months, we moved back to our old house.

The year after the fire, missionaries from International Teams Philippines came to Balic-Balic. Some of them lived in our community in order to plant a church. My mother was the first to become a Christian. My sister and I followed. We used to be members of a cult church in the community before we became Christians. They did not believe that Jesus was God, the women sat separately from the men inside the church, and they required that you give the ten percent of your income. They also believed that the physical church would go up to heaven during the rapture, and so when the rapture came everybody would need to hurry up and get inside the building. For this reason, the buildings all have the same "rocket" shape.

Life was really hard when we were growing up. My parents fought so loudly that everyone in the neighborhood could hear them. I would be afraid to go out-

side of our house sometimes because of the humiliation from the past night's argument. But there was one thing I was excited about in my life growing up, and that was coming to know Jesus. I was excited to learn more about him through Sunday school. The missionaries that taught me, and that had lived in our community, had a big impact on my life. They showed Jesus' character very vividly. I remember one time both my parents abandoned us kids for a week because they were fighting. The missionaries took care of us for that whole week.

After high school I did not think that I would be able to go to college. At the time, I was thinking that if I had the chance to go to college I wanted to go to a Bible college to become a missionary. God was really taking care of me because, by his grace, I was able to enroll on the last allowable day in a college near where I lived. Somebody from the United States, who was a friend of the missionaries, visited our community for a week and he decided to support me for one year of my study, which allowed me to enroll. After the first year, I was able to get a scholarship for two years. It was the fourth year of college that was very trying for me in terms of financial needs. But I would always pray for God's provision, and he was very faithful and on time in providing for my tuition needs. Since we had very little money and I needed some for transportation, I would often go to school without eating. But God took care of me through one of my classmates. She would ask me if I had had breakfast yet or if I had eaten lunch, and she would buy food for me. If we needed to pay for something in the class like test papers and I did not have money, she would pay for mine. Despite the fact that she got her money from her mother's store without asking, she was a great blessing to me. Even though life was hard because we were poor, knowing Jesus and having hope in him kept me going so that I could finish college.

I married an American man who was committed to serving the poor. Instead of using my degree and my marriage to escape my community, we chose to stay in Balic-Balic to serve God there. People sometimes asked me why I came back to Balic-Balic and lived like a poor person when I could have had a better life in the United States. I told them that I wanted to share with them the hope that I found in God through Jesus. Being poor is a hard thing, but it is miserable to be poor and not know God. With God, even when one is poor, life becomes hopeful and full of joy.

Ema's life is a great example of how Jesus is a blessing to the poor, both in the joy he gives and the transformation he offers. In 2008, Balic-Balic, the fifty-year-old squatter community along the train tracks in which Ema and her husband Aaron lived, was destroyed by the government. Thousands of people were displaced. Many had lived their entire lives in that community. Ema and Aaron moved to another poor community in Manila and started a new church, where they continue to help us train our new staff and interns.

Poverty is never looked on positively in the Scripture, but the poor are. Being poor, therefore, should not carry negative connotations with it. In 2 Corinthians 8:9, Paul said that Jesus became poor so that we might be made rich. Paul uses poverty as a way to capture Jesus' incarnation, his humble upbringing, his trials on earth, and his persecution and death. Jesus gave up his wealth and comfort so that we could come into the kingdom of true riches. He also identifies himself with the poor, as in the parable of the sheep and the goats in Matthew 25. Jesus' self-sacrifice is central to his character as God, and so, therefore, is his poverty. It is easy to think about the wealth of God: he is the Great Father of the prodigal son with more resources than can be imagined. But Jesus is also the Poor One in that he understands humility, simplicity, suffering, oppression, and want.

Jesus chose to be poor, and because of that all who are poor in this world can know that he understands their suffering—and also that in their poverty, they are like the creator of the universe.

10

CROSSING THE CHASM

*Besides all this, between you and us a great chasm
has been fixed, so that those who might want to
pass from here to you cannot do so, and no one can
cross from there to us.*

—Luke 16:26

IN 1993, I CO-LED A SUMMER PROJECT IN AN INNER CITY
church, which now happens to be our home church. One
night my future wife and I were supposed to help out at a
homeless shelter a half hour away in Pasadena. My wife
had been a regular volunteer there for quite some time,
and we had gone to the shelter together before. Our du-
ties were to wash people's clothes and spend the night, so
that if the person in charge had to deal with some emergency, there was someone else still on site. We never got
much sleep because the man in charge was an incredible
snorer. At the last minute, my wife had to back out. Neither

of us remembers why, but what I do remember is that I did not want to go without someone else. I have never liked new social situations and was particularly leery of going to hang out with a bunch of homeless people I did not know. I tried to get out of it, but my wife reminded me that if I did not go it would be a hardship for that ministry. Reluctantly, and maybe a little angrily, I made the drive out to Pasadena.

But something happened when I got there. I met people, not homeless people or poor people, just people. This particular shelter was for recovering drug addicts and alcoholics whose problems had landed them on the street. They were part of a program that gave them shelter and helped them with their addictions, and as a result they were pretty in touch with their problems and weaknesses. They were the most humble yet hopeful people I have ever been around. We discussed numerous topics as I waited for loads of laundry to be washed and dried. We talked about their lives: what they had been before their addiction and what they hoped they could become. They were so real. There was no pretense, no deception. They were at peace with their deep flaws and honest about the costs of their mistakes, and in addition to this, they were so grateful that I was there serving them. Everyone thanked me at some point in the night. They were such a blessing to me, and I almost missed it all.

The rich man had a choice: he could have chosen to go out to the gate and relate to Lazarus. I mentioned in Chapter 7 that he was guilty of two sins: he lived an indulgent lifestyle and he failed to care for his poor brother. Certainly there was a chasm between his house and his gate, between him and the poor man. It separated the world of wealth and comfort from that of poverty and torment. It separated the lives of the privileged, the respected, and the successful from that of the struggling, the rejected, and the "failures." It would not have been easy to cross such a chasm even if he had wanted to. What would his friends and family have said? What would it have cost him in time, money, and emotional energy? It would not have been easy, but it was a chasm he could have crossed had he chosen to. In contrast, the great eternal chasm cannot be crossed by choice.

The rich man was held responsible because he had the power to act and yet failed to do so. Lazarus had no such power. He could not have gone to the house of the rich man seeking reconciliation or demanding that the rich man care for him. Instead, he was forced to beg for mercy from God and passersby. It was the rich man's responsibility to go out and welcome Lazarus into his home. What this teaches us is that if we have the power to cross a particular chasm, we are obligated to do so since those on the other side likely do not have the same ability. We cannot wait for the poor to come to us.

In Matthew 25, Jesus tells a parable about his second coming. At that time, he said, the Son of Man will gather all the nations together and then separate them like a shepherd separates the sheep from the goats. Separating the sheep from the goats may have been a more expert task than we think of it now. In the United States, sheep and goats do not look very similar; even those of us who grew up in an urban center could separate them. However, I have been in countries near the Middle East, and they look a lot more alike there. It would be hard to tell them apart from a distance. According to Jesus, the distinguishing feature of the sheep—those who receive the kingdom—is that they fed Jesus when he was hungry, gave him something to drink when he was thirsty, welcomed him when he was a stranger, clothed him when he was naked, took care of him when he was sick, and visited him when he was in prison. At first his listeners are confused: they never saw Jesus in those conditions. But Jesus responds, "Truly I tell you, just as you did it to one of the least of these who are members of my family, you did it to me" (Matt 25:40). Jesus then said that the recognizable feature of the goats is that they never did any of those things for Jesus. Because they did not care for the least among them, they did not care for Jesus. The sheep go on to eternal life and the goats go on to eternal punishment.

It is interesting that neither group—the metaphorical sheep and goats—sees Jesus himself in the hungry, thirsty, stranger, etc. The sheep group did not take care of the poor *because* they believed they were serving their Savior in their destitute brothers and sisters; they simply lived like the Savior. They loved people, particularly those who were suffering. But we know that Jesus does identify himself with these hurting people because of this parable. I like the way the NRSV translates the phrase "members of my family" because that is Jesus' point: he identifies with hurting people because they are part of his family, which fits well with the parable of the father and the lost son. It seems reasonable that the father would feel appreciation for anyone who decided to care for his younger son in his suffering, and it is reasonable that he would see it as an act done to him since his son is an extension of himself. As a parent, any kindness done to my daughter is in some way done also to me because of my love for her and my connection to her. Jesus cares very deeply about the suffering of his brothers and sisters—he feels their pain—and so any blessing done to them he considers as done to himself.

We might prefer if Jesus had said that what divided the sheep and the goats was that one group had faith in him as their Savior, went regularly to church, read the Bible, prayed every day, and refrained from things like swearing and drinking—but he did not. The marks of the sheep are various forms of service to the destitute. I do believe that we are only saved by faith, but if our faith is not making us look more like sheep, then we have to question what we truly have faith in. We may believe that Jesus is our Savior, but we still have to choose to follow him. Both groups in the parable had a choice: to love the needy or to ignore them. The same choice lies before us: we must choose to act in love toward others; we must cross the chasms that separate us from those in need.

Earlier, I mentioned our friends Tom and Bree Hsieh. There was a point when Tom was making two hundred thousand dollars a year, but had decided—with Bree—

to live on forty thousand dollars and give the rest away. He would show up to meetings and fancy dinners in his beaten-up Geo. Once, he pulled up to a five star hotel for a meeting and handed his keys to the valets, who looked at his car and started laughing. He joined them. Tom and Bree also relocated to a poor, violent community. Tom was once the first person on the scene of a shooting that took place in front of their apartment—he was with the victim as he died. After that, his wife made him promise not to go outside until after the shooting had stopped. For a period of time, they took in a teenage girl whose mother was killed in a car accident and whose father was in jail. They also took in an entire family of five who were struggling to be free of past gang connections and needed help until they could find stable housing and employment.

What is particularly remarkable is that Tom is the eldest son of a Taiwanese immigrant family. As a college student, he began to wrestle with the radical demands of the gospel to love people sacrificially and generously—even at the expense of his studies. His parents were not pleased. Tom led his father through a Bible study of the widow's two mites to help him understand what God was calling him to. Instead of understanding, his father became enraged that God would require so much of those who followed him. Tom knew that it was not the sacrifice of money that his father was concerned about, but the sacrifice of his son in whom he had invested his hopes and ambitions. He disowned Tom on the spot and swore that he would not pray, read the Bible, or go to church ever again. He was an elder in a church at the time. Many people in

Tom's home church, including the pastor, encouraged him to submit to his parents and make his studies his priority so that he would be better equipped to serve God in the long run. Tom responded that he wanted to honor his father and mother, and he believed that the best way to do that was to trust God and be obedient to his commands. Jesus had called him to follow him, how could he turn back now?

Over time, Tom's relationship with his father was restored. The crisis caused his father to struggle with what it meant to be a follower of Jesus. When he was reinstated as an elder in the church, Tom's father honored the role his son had played in his life. "Several years ago I left the church and the faith," he said, "because my son had made some radical decisions about following God in his life that I disapproved of. I am not proud of how I responded. But I'm glad that my son chose to be obedient to God. Today, I have a deeper and more real relationship with God than I had before, because of my son's decisions." Tom wept at the service.

You have to make a conscious choice to cross a chasm. It does not happen by accident or good intentions. There are often costs. There are a number of choices that need to be considered in order to help the poor. First, we need to decide to make our needy brothers and sisters a priority in our schedules. When my wife, Lisa, was on staff with InterVarsity Christian Fellowship, she decided to volunteer regularly at the homeless shelter I mentioned earlier. At the time, this seemed like a costly decision. When we were working with IVCF, we poured a lot of hours into our students, and it felt difficult to take time out to be involved in another ministry off campus. But we had to go off campus to spend time with the poor because most everyone on campus was fairly well off. However, my wife was committed to serving the poor, so she took students with her to the shelter, thus using it as another way to be with and influence young people.

If we want to be in relationship with people from other classes, we need to create space in our schedules and go where they are. Short-term missions are a good way to realize this. I do not believe short-term trips accomplish much in terms of furthering a particular ministry, though they can be a great help to short-term projects. Their real value, instead, is in introducing the non-poor to people living in very different circumstances, so that they might gain a greater understanding of the challenges the poor face. Every American Christian would benefit from living in an international slum for a couple of weeks.

We Have a Choice Over Where We Live.

If we decide we must be in an affluent neighborhood, we limit our exposure to our poorer family members. Not everyone needs to relocate to poorer neighborhoods, but I think more should. We do have to be careful not to overrun inner city areas, inadvertently gentrifying them and forcing out the very people we came to build relationship with. We also have to be careful not to create communities of relocated people who do not really interact with the neighborhood and its indigenous leaders. But I do believe that most areas benefit from socio-economic—and ethnic—diversity. While I may at times be critical of the middle-class, in truth, it has some good values. I appreciate that middle-class neighborhoods expect that people will throw their beer bottles in trashcans and not on the sidewalk, that they will not deface other people's property, and that they will not rob or kill their neighbors—these are qualities worthy of appreciation.

Middle-class people generally respect order and believe people should obey the law. In poorer communities, people who are victimized sometimes feel that if they get away with something, it merely makes up for other ways they have been injured. The fact that something is illegal is not as great a deterrent as it is in more affluent neighborhoods, since many people are doing something against the rules, including the powers that be. A young woman who lives next door to us recently opined to my wife, "Everyone in the neighborhood is into something, Lisa, even the people you think aren't into anything." Middle-class people also tend to expect high quality school systems and that local government and the police will serve the people. These are all good values that poorer communities could benefit from. Mind you, the middle-class does not have a monopoly on such values. There are many poor people with the same values, but those who create chaos often overrun them. The dysfunctional systems around them seem daunting and impervious to reform, leaving people with little hope for change. Rather than seek to confront these systems, those with the strongest values for a healthy society usually attempt to escape them if they can.

Therefore, I think it is good for more affluent people to be neighbors with poorer people. I used to live in a very nice middle-class community, and my neighbors were quite private and unfriendly; they spent their time running from one event to another and had little desire to know me. In contrast, my poorer neighbors are around a great deal; they hang out in front of their houses and socialize for hours. It is easy to walk up and down the street and be invited to sit down and talk. Life is less harried, and it feels more like a community. Where we choose to live will determine what kind of relationships we can have with people who live differently than we currently do.

We Have a Choice Over Where We Will Worship.

In earlier times, people remained in the denomination they were born into. Presbyterians went to the Presbyterian Church, Baptists to the Baptist Church, Methodists to the Methodist Church, etc. Of course now many Protestants decide where they want to go based upon whether they like a particular church, its worship style, its preaching, and its theology. In some ways, this may be healthier since it breaks down denominational divisions, but because of this, the church has become more of a consumer product. We attend the churches we agree with, that serve our needs and make us happy. This can give us a misconception that the local church is about consumption rather than participation.

The Catholic Church divides itself geographically. If you live in a certain area, or parish, you are part of a particular church. Of course, there are exceptions to this rule—I have plenty of Catholic friends who go to churches in different communities because they like one particular church over another—but I appreciate their model as a whole. When you base a church on geography, it has a greater chance of diversity, given that the geography is diverse. The Church is also more about the community than the commodity.

Protestant churches need to find ways to be more community conscious. One of the things we have tried to do in our own church is make it neighborhood-oriented. We have members who live outside our city—and they are no less a part of our church body—but we think of ourselves as serving our surrounding neighborhood and city. When we started making changes in the orientation of the church, a lot of people left; the people who stayed were the youngest and the oldest. It was not that the older generation loved the changes being made; they were just loyal to their church and cared more about its continued existence in the community than what they personally got out of it. It was a testimony to me that church is about something larger than our experience of it: it is about a commitment to a people and a place that transcends the individual. I have nothing against young churches (Servant Partners is, after all, a church-planting ministry), but the fact that our church is 130 years old reminds me that many have ministered in the community long before me and, God willing, many will continue to minister long after me.

A number of years ago, David and Ruth became members of our congregation. They are both university professors in Southern California. They live in a middle-class community but wanted to be in a church that was working to make a difference among the poor. Our church service is not outstanding: we do not have any paid staff to run a myriad of programs for children and adults, and we have our fair share of conflicts and problems. There are a handful of Asian Americans, but we are certainly not the Korean-American church that David and Ruth had grown up in and were used to. Despite all this, they decided to worship with us in order to be drawn into a different world. Through our church, David and Ruth met an elderly African American woman who suffered from numerous ailments and struggled to thrive financially. They befriended her and cared for her, often picking her up at her apartment and bringing her to church.

There is an African American church south of us that I used to work with in the summers. The congregation was almost entirely black, though mixed socio-economically. There was one white man who was married to a black woman and one affluent, older white couple. The elderly couple had started attending the church many years earlier as a way to support the young congregation financially, and they had decided to stay. There was nothing culturally black about them—no two people could have been whiter—but they chose to be a part of a different culture, a different worship experience than the one they had grown up with. The church welcomed and loved them for who they were. It was rare to see people of that generation make such a decision. If where we live does not bring us into relationship with poor people, then we should consider worshipping in a place that does.

I would challenge us all to reflect on where we live and worship, but there are also ways we can be involved in the lives of people in different economic situations than we are without relocating. For the past number of years, I have been involved in organizing in various forms: you can organize neighborhoods and also institutions like churches and non-profits. The basic premise is to bring people together to identify and solve their own problems as well as create positive efforts for change in a community. This is particularly important for the poor since they are often treated as if they are ignorant. People often come in from the outside and try to solve their problems for them. As my friend Bob Linthicum says, they are told to hold still while we do good to them. The poor know what needs to be changed, and usually they have some idea of how to do it. It is incredibly important that disenfranchised people come to believe that they have the power to transform their own lives and their own community.

I am a local leader with the Industrial Areas Foundation, which is one of the largest and oldest organizing efforts in the country. One of the things I most appreciate about organizing is that it brings very different people together with the intention of hearing each other's stories. It is easy to abstract the poor, to categorize them neatly into conceptual boxes, but when we hear their stories they become people, not statistics. It may be easy to demonize undocumented immigrants in the abstract, but it is hard to de-monize someone you have sat face to face with, listening to their story of how and why they moved without waiting for the proper paperwork. Together, we have worked on a variety of issues, including saving people's homes from foreclosure, helping immigrant parents have access to volunteering at their children's schools, job creation, and closing down a store front that was selling drugs in the community. The battle with the waste transfer station was one of our largest local organizing efforts. For middle-class churches and student groups that want to be involved in social justice, this is one of the easiest ways to come into contact with people and their struggles. I believe that one of the best tools for producing social change—both do-mestically and internationally—is helping the poor facilitate the transformation themselves.

In his book *Walking with the Poor*, Bryant Myers ex-plains that all relationships—those between people and God, people and people, and people and nature—have become broken because of Adam and Eve's sin.[1] He later cites Jayakumar Christians' argument that this brokenness between people is made manifest in how the rich tend to perceive themselves as little messiahs whose job it is to save those they perceive as less gifted, while the poor tend to think of themselves as less valuable than others.[2] This reality—of how the rich and poor perceive themselves and each other—is essential for this discussion on how to best cross the chasms that separate us.

I keep being drawn back to a story found in Numbers

13 and 14. In chapter 13, Moses sends twelve spies to check out the land that God had promised to the descendants of Abraham. They had recently come out of slavery in Egypt and crossed the Red Sea (some translations say "Reed Sea") in dramatic fashion. The twelve examined the land for forty days, and when they returned, they reported that it indeed lived up to God's description. But what God had failed to mention was that there were now giants living there. Though it was a land "flowing with milk and honey," they thought there was no way they would be able to conquer the land and make it their own.

Caleb and Joshua were the only dissenters. While they did not dispute that there were great warriors in the land, they were convinced God would lead them to victory. The other ten started to spread a bad report of the land to the rest of the community. They said they looked like grasshoppers compared to the inhabitants of the land and, they added, "So we seemed to them." In other words, they felt small compared to the natives, and they believed the natives thought they looked small as well. In reality, there is no indication that any of the natives felt that way at all. In fact, when Joshua sent spies into the land a second time, after a forty-year detour, Rahab told them that the inhabitants were deeply afraid of the Israelites, partly because of what God had done for them at the Red Sea forty years earlier. The inhabitants never considered them as grasshoppers. The Israelites projected their own feelings of inferiority onto the giants in the land.

It is completely understandable that these recently liberated Israelite slaves would have had a hard time shaking off a low self-view. Unfortunately, they believed that because of who they were, God could not do anything for or with them. I have found this to be very reflective of how the poor often consider themselves: they sometimes have a grasshopper mentality toward the rich giants in the land because of the oppression they have experienced. It can take a long time to break this self-image; it took the Israelites forty years of wandering in the wilderness before the nation was ready to trust God to bring them into the land.[3] It is not enough to simply end the poor's oppression in order to heal their self-perception. Healing requires time. It also requires that the rich and powerful repent of the ways they continue to reinforce the poor's feelings of inferiority by acting like messiahs in the lives of the poor.

Recently, I was talking to one of our partners in Bangkok, Kaew, about the land rights movement she was a part of. For the past several years, she had worked to help a displaced squatter community acquire land on which to build permanent homes. She had met with government officials on numerous occasions. When I asked her what enabled her to believe she could stand up for this community's rights and be taken seriously, she said that the group organizing the effort had taught her and the others that just because they were poor, they were not worth less than the government officials. They did not need to grovel or beg them for the things they wanted. As citizens, they had a right to demand that the government respond.

The organization Kaew was working with is secular, comprised mostly of Buddhists, but it was better at helping the poor experience empowerment than many Christian ministries I have seen. The Christian rich often do not know how to help the poor in ways that do not reinforce the grasshopper mentality. The poor need to know that God is powerful enough to work in them and through them, and they do not need the rich undermining that confidence. Generosity helps us break the power of *Mammon* in our lives, but we need to be generous in ways that do not reinforce the grasshopper mindset.

A friend of mine from Kenya shared a story with me of a man who was walking by a river and noticed a woman drowning. Immediately, he jumped in and rescued her. On the following day, he was walking by the same river and noticed that a man was drowning. Again, he jumped in and saved him. On the third day, he was walking by the river and there was yet another woman drowning that he needed to rescue. After he rescued her, he decided to go up river to discover why so many people were falling into the river in the first place. What he found was a broken and treacherous bridge, so he decided to fix the bridge.

The ultimate task for us is fixing the bridge that causes people to fall into poverty in the first place. We have already discussed some systemic issues, but it is crucial that we understand that part of the brokenness is that people do not believe they can fix the bridge themselves. They may be waiting for someone else to come along and fix it, or they may be so busy trying not to drown that they do not have the luxury of reflecting on a building strategy.

But in order for people to become self-reliant in a healthy way, they must get to a point where they are able to assess the causes of their drowning and work to solve the problem.

The story of Nehemiah is a great example of this. Nehemiah was the cupbearer to the king of Persia—a powerful position.[4] However, when he heard how the walls of Jerusalem were still broken down, leaving the city vulnerable, he asked the king to send him back to his homeland with the resources to rebuild the walls. Once there, he surveyed the damage and called the leaders of the people together. They all decided that it was time to rebuild, and everyone set out to work on a piece of the wall nearest to their own homes. With the resources Nehemiah brought with him, they were able to rebuild the walls in fifty-two days despite some discouragement from the surrounding powers that wanted to keep them vulnerable. The walls had lain in ruins for 141 years, but were rebuilt in a mere fifty-two days.[5] Why did it take so long for them to rebuild? Though the resources were helpful, the real problem was that the people were broken, not just the walls.

Rebuilding a people takes more time than rebuilding a wall, but that should be our ultimate goal. We need to support programs and ministries that enable the poor to learn to reflect critically on their situations so that they can take responsibility for their communities and their lives. It may mean first creating enough stability in people's lives so that they have some space to learn to think this way. While they may still need some outside vision and resources to get the job done, the focus has to be investing in the people. This is why I have spent so much time emphasizing the importance of relationship: when people start to believe that God can work in and through them, significant change can happen.

Ora lives in the community we work with in South Africa. A few years ago, he started a computer literacy program for the community center there. One day, an "expert" hired by the community center came in unannounced and tore apart his program, directing him to make changes. Ora could have been completely discouraged by the encounter; he could have submitted to the outsider even though he did not agree with her critique. Instead, he decided to take his program out from under the community center's supervision and develop it the way he felt he needed to. This may seem like a small thing, but it was revolutionary: he decided that he would not be disempowered by those who supposedly were trying to help him. He took responsibility for himself and his work. He kept the program in the community center, but paid rent for the space and forbade the center from promoting it as their own, which they continually attempted to do. His program is now flourishing.

Ora has developed a healthy value for his own work and contribution. He has become a leader that can represent his community and its best interests without being dependent on unhealthy relationships. We have to find and invest in the Oras among the poor, as they will be much better equipped to bring the kind of transformation their communities need.

Part of our healing as people—not only as individuals, but also as a kingdom body—is the reconciliation of the rich and the poor. The rich need to give up their trust in *Mammon* as a tool of self-justification, and the poor need to know that they are created in the image of God and have gifts to offer even the rich. This may be the most important reason we need to push back from the table, take off the fine clothes, and go out to the gate where Lazarus lies. We who are rich need real relationships with our poor brothers and sisters for our sake as well as for theirs.

11

THE BROTHERS AND MOSES

He said, "Then, father, I beg you to send him to my father's house—for I have five brothers—that he may warn them, so that they will not also come into this place of torment." Abraham replied, "They have Moses and the prophets; they should listen to them." He said, "No, father Abraham; but if someone goes to them from the dead, they will repent." He said to him, "If they do not listen to Moses and the prophets, neither will they be convinced even if someone rises from the dead."

—Luke 16:27-31

BECAUSE OF MY WORK, I SPEND A SIGNIFICANT AMOUNT OF TIME in international slums, at least significantly more than the average American, and when I return from my trips, I am often struck by how nice our life is. Our house seems spacious, our décor extravagant. There are no large holes in our walls where vermin can easily enter. We own some art and a couple decorative items. Our daughter has her own room and does not need to sleep in the same bed as us. Our kitchen and bathroom have hot and cold running water, and we can easily heat our home in the winter and cool it in the summer. After seeing the deprivation of others, I become aware of what luxuries these are.

The opposite occurs when I spend time in the homes of wealthier people. Suddenly our house seems small at twelve hundred square feet. We share one bathroom; the carpet is worn because we cannot afford to replace it. When my extended family of about ten people comes for holidays, we have to squeeze around our small dining table. We cannot all fit into the living room, and there is no place for the kids to go and watch television while the adults talk. In times like these, I become envious of having greater space to host people.

It is funny how our company colors our perceptions of our possessions. When poorer people visit us I am embarrassed about our wealth, and when richer people come I am self-conscious about our poverty. A few years ago, I was talking with Anathi, who, at that time, lived in a squatter community outside of Johannesburg. His house had no running water or electricity, and his family had to use a public toilet. He asked me if I lived in what we called a ghetto. "Yes," I replied, "but if you saw it you would think it was pretty nice." The company we keep often determines what we consider luxurious, and what we consider luxurious might also determine the company we keep. Those of us with great possessions are likely to have relationships with people of similar lifestyles. Relating only to other wealthy people affirms our lifestyle choices and dulls us to the gospel's challenge to beware the dangers of wealth. The same was true for the rich man.

Once the rich man came to the realization that no one could aid him in his distress, his thoughts turned to his five surviving brothers. Apparently, they had been living the same lifestyle that he had with little concern for the poor in their midst. If Lazarus could go and warn them, he reasoned, maybe they would escape his fate. It is curious that he was able to be concerned for his blood brothers, but not his fellow son of Abraham, Lazarus. Like the older son in the prodigal parable, he did not see Lazarus as his brother. The problem was not that he was incapable of compassion or love; he had just drawn a line between those he considered his brothers and those he did not.

Joachim Jeremias argues that this story should be called the Parable of the Six Brothers.[1] Jesus' inclusion of the five other brothers is not story filler—they are the object of the parable. Unlike their brother whose fate is fixed, they were still able to change their lives. It must be significant that there is not just one other brother. If Jesus were trying to make the point that the rich man, now convicted of the errors of his ways, wanted to warn those he loved, the story would only need for him to have one brother. But the fact that Jesus says there were five remaining brothers emphasizes that the rich man was just one of many who had chosen to live the way he had. His entire family had created a lifestyle culture that was in conflict with the instruction of God.

Since Jesus is speaking to the Pharisees, it seems reasonable that he intends the brothers to represent them (though not only them), just as the older brother represents them in the parable in Luke 15. The Pharisees had created a similar culture of blessing extravagant living at the expense of the poor, and like the five remaining brothers, they can still change the course of their lives. It is not determined on which side of the chasm they will land, but ending up on Abraham's side would require repenting of their current lifestyles.

At this point in the parable it is clear how this teaching connects to Jesus' challenge to the Pharisees about their self-justification. Like the teaching on divorce and remarriage, it is they, not Jesus, who are breaking the Law with their love of money and disdain for the poor. They know what God requires. They just do not want to do it.

Abraham's response to the rich man's request was devastating: sending Lazarus to warn the brothers would be fruitless because they had already been thoroughly warned by Moses and the prophets, whom they had chosen to ignore. They did not suffer from a lack of knowledge; they suffered from a lack of a desire to act on that knowledge.[2] The rich man seems to agree that the teachings of Moses and the prophets is not enough; however, he argued, someone rising from the dead would get their attention. Such a person could tell them what happened to their brother because of his sin. *That* they would listen to.

No, Abraham said. If their hearts were not open to Moses and the prophets, then someone rising from the dead would not change anything.

Even as Jesus tells the Pharisees there will not be any warnings from the grave, by telling the story, he does in fact warn them. The story seems so condemning, but it is actually an extension of his mercy, since the warning holds within it the possibility of repentance. In reality, God's threat of judgment is always an aspect of his mercy because his intention is to help us choose life. Jesus could have walked away leaving the Pharisees, the rich—and us—to learn our lesson the way the rich man did, but instead he gave us a glimpse into the afterlife.

One December, I was watching an animated version of Charles Dickens' A Christmas Carol, and it struck me that the author might have been influenced by the parable of the rich man and Lazarus. In Dickens' story, Ebenezer Scrooge is visited by the ghost of his late partner, Jacob Marley, who warns him of the fate that awaits him in the afterlife if he does not repent of his greed and disregard for the poor. Marley, weighed down by the chains he now bears, bemoans his cursed situation. Scrooge cannot believe that his former partner is being tormented this way because he was "always a good man of business" in his life, suggesting that he believes that this is the ultimate virtue. In one of the most powerful sections of the book, Marley corrects Scrooge's understanding of "business":

"Business!" cried the Ghost, wringing its hands again. "Mankind was my business. The common welfare

*was my business; charity, mercy, forbearance, and
benevolence, were all my business. The dealings of
my trade were but a drop of water in the comprehensive ocean of my business!"*

Marley had wasted his life in the quest for financial success and had missed its true purpose. Sadly, his warning is
not enough. Scrooge requires the visit of three other ghosts
before he is willing to deal with his own misguided life. It
is a scary story, but one ultimately about mercy as well.
The threat of eternal judgment and the knowledge that his
death would only bring others joy is mercy for Scrooge—
because it leads to his repentance.

Though the rich man in the parable does not get a ghost
to warn his brothers, in a way, he does get what he asks
for. We—his metaphorical brothers and sisters—are able
to see the consequences of a life of indulgence and greed
that he wanted his brothers to see. There might also be
note of foreshadowing in these verses as Jesus is likely
talking in a veiled way about his own death and resurrection.[3] If the rich are not convinced by Jesus' warnings now,
even his resurrection is not going to change their minds. In
this way, Jesus differs from Dickens. This parable serves as
a warning, but Jesus does not appear to believe that visits
from the grave will change a hardened heart. People hear
what they want to hear. If their hearts are open to the commands of God, there will be no surprises in eternity; if they
are not open, no amount of miracles is going to change
their response.

By referencing Moses and the prophets, Jesus indicates

that he is not saying anything they have not heard before. God's command to be concerned for one's poor neighbor is clearly revealed throughout the writings of the Hebrew Bible. The rich man was condemned not by Jesus' new teaching, but by what was written in the Hebrew Scripture. The Pharisees might dismiss Jesus, but they cannot as easily dismiss the tradition they have based their lives upon. Up to this point, I have avoided citing numerous Hebrew Bible passages, but now it will be helpful to reflect on a few key passages to get a sense of what Jesus was building upon.

By "Moses," Jesus meant the Torah, or the Pentateuch—the first five books of the Bible.[4] "The prophets" refers to the writings of the prophets that make up the second part of the Hebrew Bible. The Torah and the prophets were read every week in the synagogue, which is where the brothers would have had an opportunity to "listen" to them.[5] For the remainder of this chapter, I want to look at some excerpts from the Torah as they include the blueprint for God's vision for the people of Israel. In them, we see the community of God as he intended it.

Exodus 22:21-26

You shall not wrong or oppress a resident alien, for you were aliens in the land of Egypt. You shall not abuse any widow or orphan. If you do abuse them, when they cry out to me, I will surely heed their cry; my wrath will burn, and I will kill you with the sword,

*and your wives shall become widows and your chil-
dren orphans. If you lend money to my people, to
the poor among you, you shall not deal with them as
a creditor; you shall not exact interest from them. If
you take your neighbor's cloak in pawn, you shall restore it before the sun goes down; for it may be your
neighbor's only clothing to use as cover; in what else
shall that person sleep? And if your neighbor cries
out to me, I will listen, for I am compassionate.*

Some of the very earliest instructions given to the
Israelites dealt with protecting the vulnerable: particularly foreigners, widows, and orphans. God reminds the
people of Israel that they, too, had been aliens in a foreign land and should remember what it was like being
mistreated by the Egyptians. His concern for the widow
and orphan is even greater: if people oppressed them and
they cried out to him, God would have the oppressors
fall to the sword, thus causing their wives and children to
become similarly vulnerable. It is a very strong reaction—
but a just one. Those who oppress the vulnerable end up
sharing their fate. In effect, God became the husband to
the widow and the father to the orphan in his protection
of them.

Orphans and widows were among the most vulnerable
to economic hardship and exploitation. This is evidenced
by the numerous passages in the Hebrew Bible referencing the need to insure their protection (Deut 10:18, 14:29,
Prov 15:25, Isa 1:23, 10:2, Jer 7:6, 22:3, Zech 7:10, Mal
3:5). This theme was not lost on James. We have already

noted that he writes that the definition of pure religion is caring for orphans and widows and keeping oneself unstained by the world (Jas 1:27). James understood that protecting such people was central to a relationship with the living God. Certainly that idea was formed not only by his relationship with Jesus, but also by his reading of the Torah. God made it clear centuries earlier that he expected the nation of Israel to imitate his heart and take on the role of husband and father to those who had lost them.

Exodus 22 continues with instructions not to charge interest and to return a cloak in the evening to a person who gave it as a pledge (essentially this meant the return of the collateral taken for the loan). Both of these commands are repeated several times in the Hebrew Bible and are intended to lessen the burden of becoming vulnerable: first, so that people were not driven into poverty and, therefore, into indentured slavery and, second, so that they were not forced to go without the basic necessities of life.[6] Our modern economy is so driven by debt, collateral, and interest collection that it is hard to imagine a world where such would be illegal.

However, this passage is not so much a condemnation of our current economy, or even commercial business at that time, as it is a protection for those who fell on hard times.[7] God instituted this so that people could not take advantage of other people's hardship. Lending should come out of mercy and generosity and not be used as an opportunity to make a profit off the poor. As we see in the text, these laws did not apply to foreigners but only to the Israelites, which might indicate that loans to foreigners were usually commercial in nature and not for poverty relief.[8]

In poor communities around the world, moneylenders prey upon the vulnerable. Because they have few options, the poor will pay huge interest in order to have access to larger sums of money needed to buy basic necessities or provide for unforeseen expenses. In Manila, for example, moneylenders come through the squatter communities every day and loan five pesos in exchange for six the next day, a little more than 16.5% daily interest.

In ancient times, a person's cloak needed to be returned in the evening because it would cause undue hardship for the owner to be without it during the cold of the night. It would not be moral for the borrower to suffer needlessly because of their debt. Similar laws can be found that condemn taking advantage of poor workers, whether Israelites or foreigners, and command paying poor workers at the end of the day so that they could purchase their daily needs (Deut 24:14-15). Poverty, then as now, made one vulnerable to being mistreated by employers or wealthier neighbors, and these commands reveal God's concern over this dynamic. A society in relationship with God protects the vulnerable and does not take advantage of them.

Deuteronomy 15:1-11

Every seventh year you shall grant a remission of debts. And this is the manner of the remission: ev-

ery creditor shall remit the claim that is held against a neighbor, not exacting it from a neighbor who is a member of the community, because the LORD'S remission has been proclaimed. From a foreigner you may exact it, but you must remit your claim on whatever any member of your community owes you. There will, however, be no one in need among you, because the LORD is sure to bless you in the land that the LORD your God is giving you as a possession to occupy, if only you will obey the LORD your God by diligently observing this entire commandment that I command you today. When the LORD your God has blessed you, as he promised you, you will lend to many nations, but you will not borrow; you will rule over many nations, but they will not rule over you.

If there is among you anyone in need, a member of your community in any of your towns within the land that the LORD your God is giving you, do not be hard-hearted or tight-fisted towards your needy neighbor. You should rather open your hand, willingly lending enough to meet the need, whatever it may be. Be careful that you do not entertain a mean thought, thinking, "The seventh year, the year of remission, is near," and therefore view your needy neighbor with hostility and give nothing; your neighbor might cry to the LORD against you, and you would incur guilt. Give liberally and be ungrudging when you do so, for on this account the LORD your God will bless you in all your work and in all that you undertake. Since there will never cease to be some in need on the

*earth, I therefore command you, "Open your hand to
the poor and needy neighbor in your land."*

Deuteronomy echoes much of Exodus, but expands on
its themes. Deuteronomy 15 begins with instructions that
debts were to be fully cancelled every seventh year. So, for
example, in the year 2000, 2007, 2014 and so on, every
debt would be cancelled no matter how much of it the
person had paid back. In effect, it gave people a chance to
start over. At the very longest, every seven years you could
start again debt free.[9]

If you have ever fallen into significant debt, you know
that it is one of the most depressing feelings in the world.
It takes all of your effort just to make the payments, and
you feel like you might be in the hole forever. Today, we
have access to credit cards, home equity lines of credit,
and other professional credit services to manage (or incur)
our debt, and we also have the protection of bankruptcy to
limit the damage indebtedness can do to us. The ancient
Israelites, on the other hand, had to rely on each other and
on God.

The ancients lived in a different economic reality from
most Americans today. The injury or death of a husband
or father could leave a woman or child without a provider,
which explains the need to care for the widow and orphan.
A natural disaster might wipe out your crop or livestock,
leaving you vulnerable not only in the present, but also
into the future as you would have nothing to reproduce,
no seed to plant the next year or no sheep to breed. If
this were a year where the land lay fallow (Exod 23:10-11),

you might have no income with which to purchase other necessary commodities. In any case, there is no mention in this text of the causes of the debt, only that God intended his people to be generous and give loans to each other when in need (Deut 15:7-8). There seems to be an assumption that people would start repaying the debts they incurred; however, they were not stuck in repayment forever.

People were given a second chance. Wealth was intended to be redistributed enough so that people could get back on their feet and start providing for themselves again. In such a system, some people who made loans did not get back all of their money. In fact, God warns the people in verse 9 that they should be careful not to withhold a loan because the seventh year of debt forgiveness was approaching. If a poor brother needed resources just before the seventh year, you were to give him what he needed *even* if it meant that you would have to forgive the debt in a few months and lose most of your loan. If you failed to be generous to him, he could cry out to God. This was, in essence, the filing of a legal complaint against you with God himself as the ultimate judge.[10] If such a complaint were made, God would rule against you, finding you guilty of sin.

People were required to be generous. Your poor brother had a right to your excess wealth, so much so that he could appeal to God if you failed to help him. This is consistent with the idea of stewardship that we have been discussing: the wealthy did not own their wealth, it belonged to God, and therefore, it was right for those in need to ask for it. Walter Brueggemann observed that such social transactions were never just between two parties, but were between three[11]—God was always a participant in every financial transaction.

I cannot even imagine our society working this way today. We are so convinced that what we have is rightfully ours that if we are generous, it is out of the goodness of our hearts, not because anyone has a right to what we have. Paul did tell the Corinthians they should not give under compulsion (2 Cor 9:7), which might lead us to conclude that we have the right not to give if we do not want to, but that would be misinterpreting Paul's point. As we saw in the story of Ananias and Sapphira, we do have ultimate freedom over that which God has entrusted to us, but Paul certainly expected the Corinthian church to give something. He spends much of 2 Corinthians 8-9 arguing for why the Corinthians needed to be generous. In addition, he sent Titus on ahead of him to make sure they were giving with a good spirit and not with bitterness. The main issue was not whether they would give, but whether they would get their hearts right so that they would give generously and joyfully. God makes the same argument here in Deuteronomy 15:10: the Israelites should give generously without a grudging heart.

God expected those who had more to make their wealth available to those who had less even if it meant they would not be fully repaid. Their dependence should not be upon their wealth, but upon the provision of God. If they were generous with others, God would bless them with everything that they needed (Deut 15:10). However, God seems to argue earlier that there did not need to be poor people in the first place. In Deuteronomy 15:4-5, he says, "There will, however, be no one in need among you, because the LORD is sure to bless you in the land that the LORD your God is giving you as a possession to occupy, if only you will obey the LORD your God by diligently observing this entire commandment that I command you today." In other words, if they remained faithful to the commands that had been laid out in the previous chapters, God would be so generous to them that there would be no poverty at all. If they followed his commands, God would make sure that there was enough for everyone.

How then are we to understand verse 11 where God says, apparently contradictorily, that there will always be poor people? The promise of abundant provision is contingent upon the obedience of the people. God knew that they would not keep up their end of the bargain, and as a result, there would always be poverty.[12] The commands listed in Deuteronomy 15—to be generous to the poor and forgive debts every seven years—were really safeguards so that the vulnerable were not victims of the nation's disobedience. God's ideal plan was that there would be no need in the nation of Israel, but since there would be poverty due to people's sin and disobedience, he set up a safety net of instructions that would help people out of hardship. As we have seen in the Luke 16 parables, the responsibility for the poor is put upon those who have more resources—individuals were meant to care for the needs of other individuals—

but we also see that this expectation was held corporately and was institutionalized by setting the sabbatical year.

Deuteronomy gives us a picture of God's intention for his people. Ideally, a society based upon a relationship with him would not have any poverty because he is able to provide enough for everyone if they continue to trust in him. However, since he knew that the nation could not be fully obedient, he expected that the poor and vulnerable would still need to be taken care of—first, by those with abundance lending to those in need, and second, by the periodic forgiveness of debts in order to help them out of long-term indebtedness. People were to be treated with mercy and generosity on a daily basis, and the forgiveness of debt every seven years prevented gross injustices and oppression from taking root in society.[14]

Leviticus 25:8-24

You shall count off seven weeks of years, seven times seven years, so that the period of seven weeks of years gives forty-nine years. Then you shall have the trumpet sounded loud; on the tenth day of the seventh month—on the day of atonement—you shall have the trumpet sounded throughout all your land. And you shall hallow the fiftieth year and you shall proclaim liberty throughout the land to all its inhabitants. It shall be a jubilee for you: you shall return, every one of you, to your property and every one of you to your family. That fiftieth year shall be a jubilee for you: you shall not sow, or reap the aftergrowth, or harvest the un-pruned vines. For it is a jubilee; it shall be holy to you:

you shall eat only what the field itself produces.

In this year of jubilee you shall return, every one of you, to your property. When you make a sale to your neighbor or buy from your neighbor, you shall not cheat one another. When you buy from your neighbor, you shall pay only for the number of years since the jubilee; the seller shall charge you only for the remaining crop years. If the years are more, you shall increase the price, and if the years are fewer, you shall diminish the price; for it is a certain number of harvests that are being sold to you. You shall not cheat one another, but you shall fear your God; for I am the LORD your God.

You shall observe my statutes and faithfully keep my ordinances, so that you may live on the land securely. The land will yield its fruit, and you will eat your fill and live on it securely. Should you ask, "What shall we eat in the seventh year, if we may not sow or gather in our crop?" I will order my blessing for you in the sixth year, so that it will yield a crop for three years. When you sow in the eighth year, you will be eating from the old crop; until the ninth year, when its produce comes in, you shall eat the old. The land shall not be sold in perpetuity, for the land is mine; with me you are but aliens and tenants. Throughout the land that you hold, you shall provide for the redemption of the land.

One of the more remarkable instructions in the Torah is that of Jubilee, found in Leviticus 25. At the end of seven cycles of the Sabbatical Year—in the fiftieth year—the people were to proclaim a Year of Jubilee, at which time everyone was to return to the land their family inherited when they entered the Promised Land. If you had been forced to sell your land because you had fallen on hard times, the land was returned to you, the original owner.

As in Deuteronomy 15, this allowed people to start over. Debts were to be regularly forgiven, but every fifty years you would get back the agrarian land of your family so that you could start providing for yourself again. In addition to helping people who had lost their land, this command also kept people from acquiring more and more property. There was little incentive to amass land since you would really only be renting it for the value of the crops (Lev 25:16). It kept the gap between the rich and the poor from growing.[15]

In verse 23, God says that the land should never be sold permanently because all the land really belongs to him: the people are only tenants, not owners, so they have no right to sell or buy permanently. Again we see this theme of stewardship: the land was a gift from God, and as such, God expected people to use it graciously toward one another. There is a direct connection between the Sabbatical Year's instructions to rest from labor and the Jubilee Year's economic redistribution. They were both founded upon the beliefs that God had been generous and that he was able to take care of those who trusted him. Property was a tool to provide for your needs, but it was not to be relied upon as if it were God. The Sabbatical Year and the Jubilee Year instituted a corporate trust of God over wealth. In effect, the Jubilee was a reenactment of the exodus and a reminder of God's miraculous deliverance and provision.[16]

In the Jubilee, God instituted a kind of reset button for the nation's economy. There is no clear biblical evidence that the Jubilee was ever observed, likely because of its radical requirements.[17] In Nehemiah, however, there is an example of a partial Jubilee, and we will look at that passage in the next chapter.

Leviticus 25 also contains several instructions about how to redeem, that is, buy back, land and houses. Again, the main purpose here was to give people a chance to get back what they had lost. You could buy back a piece of land at any point, and you had a year to buy back a house within a walled city; the latter would not be returned in the Jubilee, but the former would.

In verse 35, God instructs his people that if someone becomes poor and is unable to support himself, he must be given aid so that he can continue to survive. If you have the means to do so, you should take him in and care for him; you should not charge interest or sell him food at a profit. All of these commands are consistent with what we have seen in the other books of the Torah.

The Torah contains several other instructions that benefit the poor in addition to the three texts we have looked at here. A provision to let your fields, orchards, and vineyards lay fallow every seventh year was put in place in part to allow the poor access to whatever the land naturally produced (Exod 23:10-11). At every harvest, farmers were to leave some sheaves of wheat and olives in their orchards for the sake of the needy who might come by and collect them (Deut 24:19-22). The prohibitions against taking bribes in legal cases were a protection mostly for the poor (Deut 16:19). For the celebrations of the Passover and the feast of Booths, the nation was to make sure that servants, Levites, foreigners, orphans, and widows were able to participate despite their lack of resources (Deut 24:14, 17, 19, 21). Every three years, the tithe of the year's produce was supposed to be stored in the towns so that the Levites, foreigners, orphans, and widows could access it (Deut 14:28-29).

Redistribution of wealth and giving breaks to the needy were part of God's vision for society. How we apply that in our current context is complex, especially since we do not live in a theocracy. I do not think we can assume that a socialist society is nearer what God expects of his people than a free market capitalist system or vice versa, though at the same time, it is clear that God has no value for amassing wealth at the expense of the poor. A society that trusts God finds ways to redistribute wealth to those who need it so that they can get back on their feet. God expects the wealthy to help those who cannot provide for themselves. No society that has a major disparity between rich and poor can be considered consistent with the intentions for the nation of Israel, let alone the kingdom of God.

In these passages, we can see the foundation on which Jesus' parables were built. The poor were to receive special protection because of their vulnerability, and the rich were to be generous with those in need. Debts were to be cancelled, and wealth was to be periodically redistributed so that people could start over. There were some institutional measures to insure that the vulnerable were not overlooked; however, you as an individual were still responsible to meet the needs of your poor brothers and sisters around you. Failure to do these things could result in God's judgment falling upon you.

Besides the obvious avoidance of judgment, God makes three recurring arguments for why the Israelites were expected to be generous to the poor. The first was that they had been victims of injustice themselves at one point and should therefore identify with their vulnerable neighbors. Second, God liberated them from that oppression so they were indebted to his mercy and should in turn be merciful toward others. And third, the land they had been given as an inheritance was a gift of grace, not because they had done anything to deserve it. Because of this, they did not own it, but were stewards of God's gift and should therefore be generous with it. You can hear these themes in Jesus' teachings as well, and as we have seen, he raises the bar by teaching us that not only are we to loan to people, we are to give to them with no expectation of being repaid. We are to reject the gospel of *Mammon* and, instead, trust God and give generously and sacrificially.

There is plenty in the Torah to condemn the actions and inactions of the rich man. He did not lend to Lazarus or take him in; he did not redistribute his wealth or remember the past sufferings of his own people. He did not view what he had as grace from God, and he did not view himself merely as a steward of that wealth. Because he failed to do these things, the warning in the Torah was fulfilled and God's judgment came.

12

THE BROTHERS AND THE PROPHETS

He said, "Then, father, I beg you to send him to my father's house—for I have five brothers—that he may warn them, so that they will not also come into this place of torment." Abraham replied, "They have Moses and the prophets; they should listen to them." He said, "No, father Abraham; but if someone goes to them from the dead, they will repent." He said to him, "If they do not listen to Moses and the prophets, neither will they be convinced even if someone rises from the dead."

—Luke 16:27-31

SOME FRIENDS OF MINE RECENTLY DISCOVERED THAT THE WORKing conditions on many cruise ships are deplorable for those who provide menial services, such as housekeeping and waiting on tables. These people may work as many as twenty hours a day with no day off during the week, and yet their guaranteed salaries are often well below minimum wage, sometimes as little as fifty dollars a month. Cruise companies get away with this by flying under other country's flags and are therefore not subject to US labor laws. Most of these roles are filled by the poor from Asia and Latin America. If you have ever been on an international cruise, you know that there is usually a request at the end of the trip to give money to your housekeeper and waiter in a lump sum. What they do not tell you is that this is not really a tip so much as their salary. This deplorable practice is why international cruises are so much cheaper than those within the United States, where they have to adhere to our labor laws.

I have only been on one cruise in my life, and I had no idea how people were being treated. I learned about this injustice when my friends decided to help raise awareness of the nautical issue by showing up en mass in Vancouver, Canada dressed in pirate attire. With a good mixture of fun and information, they began to call attention to the practices that no one ever spoke about. You can see some of their interviews with workers if you search for "Sweatships" on YouTube.

This is an example of the role of the prophet in society and the kingdom: they make us aware of how we are straying from God and how we need to live out the kingdom in our current context. They may at times be eccentric and extreme, but often they must do so to get our attention back on what we have conveniently ignored. This was true for Israel's prophets as well. The main role of the biblical prophet was not to predict the future, as we have often been led to believe, but to call people to repentance.[1]

From time to time we grow complacent in areas of our spiritual lives, and we need to be called to wake up and change. This is what the prophets did for Israel, and this is why I have written this book. It has come out of the conviction I have experienced as I have wrestled with God's voice in Scripture.

Amos 2:6-7a

Thus says the Lord:
For three transgressions of Israel,
and for four, I will not revoke the punishment;
because they sell the righteous for silver,
and the needy for a pair of sandals—
they who trample the head of the poor into the dust
of the earth,
and push the afflicted out of the way

After Solomon's reign as king of Israel, the nation was split in two nations—the northern kingdom, referred to as Israel, and the southern kingdom, called Judah. The prophetic writing of Amos written above was against the northern kingdom, which fell completely to the Assyrians in 722 B.C.E., 135 years before the Babylonians destroyed Jerusalem in 587 B.C.E.

After criticizing the surrounding nations, including Judah, in the beginning of the book, Amos turns his attention to Israel in 2:6. The abuse and oppression of the poor seem to be the major sins of the nation,[2] and the first two accusations deal with how the courts had become corrupt, particularly toward the poor. Judges were taking bribes of silver to decide against the innocent, and the needy were being sold for a pair of shoes.[3] There are at least a couple of possible interpretations for this second image. One is that judges were not holding out for silver; they were willing to settle for footwear as bribes, which speaks to what little value they had for the poor. Another possibility is that people were selling off the poor into indentured slavery even though all they owed was the equivalent of a pair of sandals.[4] In either case, it is clear that the courts had become corrupt, and instead of protecting the poor as God desired, they had begun to oppress them.

Verse 7 deals with another aspect of their oppression, namely their utter lack of compassion on the poor. The word "trample" here is the same word that is used in Genesis 3:15 in reference to the serpent "bruising" the woman's offspring's heel and the offspring "bruising" the serpent's head.[5] People were treating the poor with the same violence they treated the serpent; they were equated to creatures worthy of being destroyed under foot. The people turned their backs on the afflicted and showed them no mercy, unconcerned about their suffering.[6] They had no compassion on their situation and felt no compulsion to assist them.

Israel denied the poor justice and felt free to treat them with disdain despite the numerous warnings against such behavior in the Torah. This was Amos' very first critique against the nation, which gives us a sense of just how serious this issue is to God. He has no tolerance for those who do not share his concern for the vulnerable. The northern kingdom fell under God's judgment partially because of this sin—a judgment from which the nation would never fully recover.

Ezekiel 22:23-31

The word of the LORD came to me: Mortal, say to it: You are a land that is not cleansed, not rained upon in the day of indignation. Its princes within it are like a roaring lion tearing the prey; they have devoured human lives; they have taken treasure and precious things; they have made many widows within it. Its priests have done violence to my teaching and have profaned my holy things; they have made no distinction between the holy and the common, neither have they taught the difference between the unclean and the clean, and they have disregarded my sabbaths, so that I am profaned among them. Its officials within it are like wolves tearing the prey, shedding blood, destroying lives to get dishonest gain. Its prophets have smeared whitewash on their behalf, seeing false visions and divining lies for them, saying, "Thus says the LORD GOD," when the LORD has not spoken. The people of the land have practiced extortion and committed robbery; they have oppressed the poor and needy, and have extorted from the alien without redress. And I sought for anyone among them who would repair the wall and stand in the breach before me on behalf of the land, so that I would not destroy it; but I found no one. Therefore I have poured out my indignation upon them; I have consumed them with the fire of my wrath; I have returned their conduct upon their heads, says the LORD GOD.

By the time of Ezekiel, numerous prophets had risen up to proclaim the impending judgment on the southern kingdom and Jerusalem. Babylon had already conquered the city and Ezekiel was among those taken into captivity, but Jerusalem's complete fall—along with the destruction of the temple—had not yet occurred.[7] This passage from Ezekiel gives us a unique perspective on the different roles of leadership within Judah's society and how the leaders abused their power and failed to work for justice.

There are four different people groups that are mentioned: princes, priests, officials, and prophets.[8] The princes of Ezekiel's time are likened to roaring lions that devour their prey. Like lions, they overpowered their victims by sheer strength and used authority and military power to take what they wanted. Instead of protecting widows, they created more widows. The priests had ceased to teach the people what was holy, leaving them ignorant of God's will. They could have spoken against the wrongs they were seeing, but they did not. The officials, who were likely financial overseers, acted like wolves: they gathered together in a pack to bring down the vulnerable in order to enrich themselves through economic exploitation.[9] The prophets had failed to point out how the people were not following God and instead falsely proclaimed that God was not displeased with them at all.[10] As a result of how these four people groups misused their power, society fell into chaos, practicing extortion, committing robbery, oppressing the poor, and mistreating the alien by denying them justice (verse 29). Their collective failure meant that Jerusalem's destruction was inevitable.[11]

It was God's intention that these people act together to see that justice was done. The political authority, the religious authority, the economic authority, and the prophetic authority were meant to help lead the nation in its pursuit of *shalom*—the wellbeing and peace of God demonstrated by everyone living in right relationship with God, each other, and creation.[12] They were supposed to lead the people into righteousness, but instead they used their authority to enrich themselves at the expense of the poor and vulnerable. Instead of holiness, they led the people into sin.

Ezekiel's description of a society that fails to do justice is still accurate today. Those who are supposed to protect sometimes use their power to dominate and oppress so that their own power can be maintained; those who are supposed to insure economic fairness often exploit people for their own financial gain; those who represent God may tell people what they want to hear rather than the uncomfortable truth which might turn people against them (or cause them to go to another church). When these systems are far from God, the poor and vulnerable are the largest victims. It is in this state that God seeks to intervene. Through the prophet Ezekiel, God declares that he is looking for someone—anyone—who would stand on behalf of the land so that he would not have to destroy it. But,

God declares, there was no such person to be found. No one would speak out for justice. No one would challenge the evil that was being done. Among all these groups, not one leader would stand up and call the people back to God. "Therefore," God continues, "I have poured out my indignation upon them; I have consumed them with the fire of my wrath; I have returned their conduct upon their heads" (Ezek 22:31).

Judgment fell upon Judah because, as a society, they did not seek God and do justice. From this we see that God is not only concerned with individual responses, corporate bodies can suffer his wrath, too.

Isaiah 58

Shout out, do not hold back!
Lift up your voice like a trumpet!
Announce to my people their rebellion,
to the house of Jacob their sins.
Yet day after day they seek me
and delight to know my ways,
as if they were a nation that practiced righteousness
and did not forsake the ordinance of their God;
they ask of me righteous judgments,
they delight to draw near to God.
"Why do we fast, but you do not see?
Why humble ourselves, but you do not notice?"
Look, you serve your own interest on your fast-day,
and oppress all your workers.
Look, you fast only to quarrel and to fight
and to strike with a wicked fist.

Such fasting as you do today
will not make your voice heard on high.
Is such the fast that I choose,
a day to humble oneself?
Is it to bow down the head like a bulrush,
and to lie in sackcloth and ashes?
Will you call this a fast,
a day acceptable to the LORD?
Is not this the fast that I choose:
to loose the bonds of injustice,
to undo the thongs of the yoke,
to let the oppressed go free,
and to break every yoke?
Is it not to share your bread with the hungry,
and bring the homeless poor into your house;
when you see the naked, to cover them,
and not to hide yourself from your own kin?
Then your light shall break forth like the dawn,
and your healing shall spring up quickly;
your vindicator shall go before you,
the glory of the LORD shall be your rearguard.
Then you shall call, and the LORD will answer;
you shall cry for help, and he will say, Here I am.
If you remove the yoke from among you,
the pointing of the finger, the speaking of evil,
if you offer your food to the hungry
and satisfy the needs of the afflicted,
then your light shall rise in the darkness
and your gloom be like the noonday.
The LORD will guide you continually,

and satisfy your needs in parched places,
and make your bones strong;
and you shall be like a watered garden,
like a spring of water,
whose waters never fail.
Your ancient ruins shall be rebuilt;
you shall raise up the foundations of many
*   generations;*
you shall be called the repairer of the breach,
the restorer of streets to live in.
If you refrain from trampling the Sabbath,
from pursuing your own interests on my holy day;
if you call the Sabbath a delight
and the holy day of the LORD honorable;
if you honor it, not going your own ways,
serving your own interests, or pursuing your
*   own affairs;*
then you shall take delight in the LORD,
and I will make you ride upon the heights of the
*   earth;*
I will feed you with the heritage of your ancestor
*   Jacob,*
for the mouth of the LORD has spoken.

One of the most well-known prophetic chapters related to poverty and justice is found in Isaiah 58. This passage was likely written to those who had returned from the Babylonian captivity to rebuild Jerusalem,[13] but instead of the comfort promised earlier in Isaiah, they found deprivation. Not much had changed since Ezekiel's time: civil and religious leaders were still seeking only their own financial gain, and the court system was likewise thoroughly corrupt.[14]

Isaiah 58 begins with God telling Isaiah to proclaim the sins of the house of Jacob. The people are confused: they have fasted and sought God, but he has not answered them. They think that they have done what is right and do not understand why God is not listening to them. But while they are fasting and supposedly seeking him, they continue to exploit their workers and quarrel with each other. They have the form of religious rigor, but seem to be missing the point of it altogether.

In verse 5 God asks, "Is [this] such the fast that I choose, a day to humble oneself? Is it to bow down the head like a bulrush, and to lie in sackcloth and ashes? Will you call this a fast, a day acceptable to the LORD?" God was not impressed by their outward religious actions—he was looking for true obedience.[15] In verses 6 and 7, he redefined fasting. True fasting was found in loosing the chains of injustice, setting the oppressed free, sharing food with the hungry, providing the poor wanderer with shelter, and clothing the naked. If the people wanted to seek God and be heard by him, they needed to become people who worked for justice and cared for the homeless and hungry. This, God insisted, is real spirituality.

While the people had all the trappings of religion, it had not led them to reconciled relationships with each other. They prayed and fasted fervently, but did not care about the poor and oppressed around them. It was as if they believed that their relationship with God had nothing to do with how they treated their neighbors.

In this passage, we see that God makes no major distinction between individual and corporate responsibility when it comes to caring for the needy. There are some very practical steps individual people need to take—provide food for the hungry, shelter for the homeless, and clothes for the naked. But there is also a call to end oppression and injustice, which would seem to imply reforming the systems that had become corrupt.

We are more individualistic than the ancients were and are prone to focus on our individual relationships with God and our individual responsibilities to him, whereas the nation of Israel and the early church had a much more corporate understanding of their faith. The people's complaint that is implied at the beginning of Isaiah 58 is a corporate one. God, they believe, is not hearing them as a people because he is not helping them as a nation. They had a corporate request of God, and his criticism is a corporate one as well. They were failing to live up to the expectations of God not only as individuals but also as a society.

Judah's sin is encapsulated at the end of verse 7. Despite their religious practices, they had turned away from their own flesh and blood. They had not seen the poor and oppressed as their family members and had not sought to love them as themselves; therefore, their corporate relationship with God was in jeopardy. They had become preoccupied with their own interests.[16]

Yet—if they changed their treatment of the poor and oppressed, God would bless them again as a people. If they indeed repented, their light would break forth like the dawn and their healing would come quickly. Their righteousness would go before them and the glory of the LORD would protect them from behind. Then they would call out to God, and he would answer, "Here I am." They would be like a well-watered garden, like a spring that never dries up. One of the greatest promises is that they would be called "the repairer of the breach, the restorer of streets to live in" (Isa 58:12). In other words, God would allow them to be the generation who rebuilt the nation that had been carried off into exile. This was their great hope, but the fulfillment of the promise was contingent on their true repentance.

Nehemiah 5

I discussed part of the book of Nehemiah earlier, but I want to return to this very rich story here. Technically Nehemiah belongs to the section in the Protestant Old Testament entitled the historical books, not the prophetic books, but I think it is a very helpful picture of how the nation of Judah responded to the critiques in Amos, Ezekiel, and Isaiah.

Nehemiah was not a prophet; he was the cupbearer to the king of Persia, Artaxerxes. His family was likely taken into exile by the Babylonians when they conquered Jerusalem. When God sent the Persians to defeat the Babylonians, allowing the nation to be released from exile several decades later, Nehemiah remained in Persia and rose in rank to become an important official in the Persian courts.[17] By the beginning of Nehemiah's story, people had started to return to Jerusalem, but the city walls had not yet been rebuilt and the city remained vulnerable to attack. When Nehemiah heard a report about this from Hanani, who had just come from Jerusalem, he wept and prayed that God would help him. He asked Artaxerxes to send him back to Jerusalem so that he could rebuild the wall. The king agreed and made Nehemiah governor of the area.

By chapter 5, the reconstruction of the wall was well underway; however, as they started to rebuild, it became apparent to Nehemiah that there were bigger problems in the community than just the wall's deterioration. There were people who were struggling to feed their families. Some had mortgaged their land and homes to buy food because of the famine. They had borrowed money to pay the king's tax and had sold their children into indentured slavery in order to meet their debts; and because they no longer owned their lands, they were powerless to get out of debt. The main people responsible for their hardship were their own nobles and officials, the very groups Ezekiel had singled out decades earlier.

Nehemiah was angry. He brought together the leaders and accused them of burdening their brothers. When they did not repent, he changed tactics.[18] He called together an assembly of all the people and publically confronted the nobles and the officials about their actions.

What particularly angered Nehemiah was that he had

been working to buy people out of slavery only to discover that his own people had been enslaving them, forcing him to buy them back again. The leaders had nothing to say; they did not defend themselves against his public accusation. Nehemiah challenged them to stop charging interest and to give the lands and vineyards they had taken—as well as all the interest they had charged up to this point— back to the people. This affected Nehemiah as well because he, too, had been lending to the people. He agreed to join them in forgiving everyone's debts. Nehemiah was aware of what God had laid out in Deuteronomy and Leviticus and applied it to the situation he was in.

When confronted by Nehemiah in front of all of the people of Jerusalem, the leaders chose to submit. Nehemiah, wanting to get their agreement "in writing" lest they change their minds later, made them take an oath before the priests to do what they had promised and then threatened them with the judgment of God if they failed to follow through. It is the closest thing to a Jubilee recorded in the Hebrew Bible. The rich actually repented (though not without a little arm twisting) and redistributed lands back to their poor brothers and sisters.

Reading Amos, Ezekiel, and Isaiah could leave us wondering if what God expected of his people in their treatment of the poor was even possible. Could the rich ever really care for the poor? Could those who benefitted from corrupt systems repent and do justice? We learn from Nehemiah that this is not only possible, it happened. For at least one brief, shining moment, the nation of Israel did justice as God willed. In the end, all it took was one man who cared about the vulnerable and challenged the community as a whole to do the same.

The restoration of Judah required a Nehemiah to stand in the gap in the wall and demand justice and holiness, but it was not wholly dependent on him; the people did the work of restoring the wall. Nehemiah provided a vision for rebuilding and the hope that it was possible—he also brought the resources of the Persian Empire—but nothing would have happened if the people had not responded to his call and done the work of rebuilding both the wall and *shalom* in their community.

I believe that there are many Nehemiahs out there today who are standing in the breach and calling us to repent and live as God wants us to. I also believe that many are listening to these men and women. Yet clearly, the American church as a whole is not. Real transformation will not happen until the people of God repent and rise up to rebuild what has broken down.

The nations of Israel and Judah came under judgment, in part, because of their treatment of the poor. God's picture of a *shalom*-centered society was clear enough from Moses and the prophets that Nehemiah, a man who grew up in a foreign land, knew how to implement it. It would have been impossible for the rich man in Jesus' parable to claim ignorance of God's intentions related to the poor and of God's displeasure toward those who violated those intentions.

As followers of Jesus we can work for a more just world, one that more closely resembles the kingdom. But our standard for the church must be even higher. Since it is the body that claims God as king, the church needs to strive to live out the kingdom and its values fully. Our world may not repent of its trust in *Mammon*, but the church should. Our world may not expect people to redistribute wealth to the poor, but the church should. We may not be able to demand that the world seek to befriend the Lazarus at their gate, but the church should require it as part of our discipleship and commitment to unity in the body of Christ. We can and should work to further the kingdom in the world, but we *must* establish it in our lives and in our Christian institutions.

When we read the prophets, it is obvious that God cares deeply for the poor and is angered by the injustice they suffer. How could the rich man who supposedly knew Abraham as his father pass by Lazarus every day and not think that judgment would one day befall him? How could he not consider him his brother when Moses and the prophets continually reminded him otherwise? How could he believe that God would hear his prayers while he turned away from his own flesh and blood? How could he miss the prophets' words about why judgment fell on the nation?

The evidence against the rich man is overwhelming. The prophets, like Moses, called out to him and his brothers every time the Scriptures were opened in the synagogue. When we look at these texts, it makes Abraham's response to him about his brothers seem less callous. They had Moses and the prophets, what more did they need?

13

NOW THAT SOMEONE HAS RISEN FROM THE DEAD

SECOND KINGS 22 RECOUNTS HOW, EIGHTEEN YEARS INTO HIS reign, King Josiah ordered that long overdue repairs be done to the temple. During the restoration, the high priest Hilkiah discovered a book of the Law—most likely a version of Deuteronomy.[1] For the first time in his life, Josiah heard the words of the book of the Law and repented for the ways the people had not held to the commands of God. He then celebrated the Passover—like it had not been celebrated since the time of the judges. When presented with the book of the Law, Josiah knew he needed to change the way he and everyone in the kingdom lived. But how could the people of the covenant have misplaced the writings in the first place? It seems inconceivable. To be an Israelite was to be a person of the Law, but there it lay in some forgotten corner of the temple, unread and unnoticed for years. How was that possible? Was it intentional or just neglectful?

Perhaps this was not as impossible as it sounds. Even

today we can misplace the Scriptures, or at least sizable chunks of it. It may be that we just read over certain texts like Luke 16 without really considering their implications for our lives, or perhaps we respond like the Pharisees, scoffing at teaching that challenges our love of money and comfort because our culture has become so disconnected from the values of the kingdom that we cannot conceive of living differently. We may even create whole theologies, perhaps also like the Pharisees, that protect us from having to be obedient in our use of wealth or in our treatment of our poor brothers and sisters. How can we be more like Josiah and less like the Pharisees?

One thing that stands out about the parable of the prodigal son in Luke 15 is that it is unfinished: we do not know what the older brother decides. Does he go into the party and embrace his estranged brother or does he return to the field angry and vindictive? Jesus was giving the Pharisees an invitation; their fate was not sealed, and they still could have responded to the Father's invitation. The parable of the rich man and Lazarus ends somewhat similarly: the fates of the five remaining brothers were not sealed either. There was still a chance that they could listen to Moses and the prophets and change the way they lived. Likewise, the Pharisees, if they truly cared about the Scriptures, could still discover the written truth and repent.

Today, we not only have Moses and the prophets, we have Jesus as well. And yet that does not seem to make living in generosity and compassion any easier. It is so hard for the American church to wrestle with this teaching because *Mammon* has so infiltrated our culture—and not only our secular culture, but our church culture as well. We may be tempted to ask if obedience is even possible.

The parable of the rich man and Lazarus is about judgment, but it is not about condemnation: the ending of the story has not been written for the brothers—or for us for that matter. Although this parable seems harsh, it is ultimately about grace, and there can be no grace without the threat of judgment. God would not be loving or good if he did not thoroughly warn us that certain choices we make will lead us toward death. It might seem counterintuitive to us, but judgment is in fact a form of grace because it is intended to cause us to choose life. We are condemned only if we choose not to respond.

I say this not as one who stands outside and condemns others, but as one who struggles with the same sins of my culture. I like nice things and desire comfort. I am often anxious about money and whether I have enough to protect my family. I have little natural compassion for my poor brothers and sisters. And, to my great shame, I am somewhere deep down tempted to believe the ugly lie that having more money or nicer things somehow makes you a more valuable person.

I have to come to Jesus regularly and repent of the ways I am hopelessly broken in this area. I have to trust that his grace is sufficient for me. But the appropriate response to such conviction is not to claim God's grace and then go on unchanged, but rather to bear fruit worthy of repentance. I need to repent of my sin, turn around, and take a step in the right direction.

Trying to follow Jesus is often scary and the costs can seem too great to bear, but it is on the road with him that we will find life. The South African missiologist, David Bosch, delivered a series of lectures collected in a little book called *A Spirituality of the Road*, where he asserts that Christians sometimes believe that in order to encounter God we need to retreat from mission, from ministry, while in fact, we encounter him on the road just as often as in retreat. "The involvement in the world," Bosch argues, "should lead to a deepening of our relationship with and dependence on God, and the deepening of this relationship should lead us to increased involvement in the world."[2] The church is called out of the world and, at the same time, sent into the world. "These are not two separate movements but one," he continues. "The idea is therefore not one of balance but rather of tension. It is not a case of the establishment of an equilibrium. Rather, the church's being called out of the world, sends her into the world; her being sent into the world calls her out of the world."[3]

My experience has been the same. I have learned much about God's character, love, compassion, justice, and mercy, as well as my own brokenness and need for healing, while seeking to love my poor brothers and sisters and seeking to see his kingdom come in this world. This ministry has brought me closer to God and made me more reliant on his grace, and although I have been made more aware of my own sin, I also hope I have become more like Jesus in the process. I had to have a neighbor in need before I could learn to love him as I love myself. Loving my enemies was always hypothetical until, working for justice, I actually developed some. Many people assume that those who desire to minister among the poor must be gifted with some exceptional compassion and mercy, but it is far more important that those of us who are weak in these areas make sure we are in places where God can develop that character in us. We will find our own healing in the healing of the world—our *shalom* in its *shalom* (Jer 29:7).

Our goal, as Paul puts it in Philippians 3:10, is to become like our Lord Jesus. Surely, this is a joy, not a horrible burden. God calls us to life, not death, no matter how much our fleshly hearts try to convince us otherwise. When we respond to Jesus' call, we cannot be certain where it will lead us. We may not be ready to emulate Zacchaeus' total repentance, but we do not need go away sad like the rich young man either. We do not have to leap over the chasm in a single bound. We just have to take the first step out onto the bridge.

So how do we begin? We may all be in different places on this journey, so let me suggest two possible phases. If you are just starting to wrestle with the issues of money and your relationship with your poor brothers and sisters, start with Phase One. Once you have acted on some of the things in Phase One, move to Phase Two. In each phase, I will identify some concrete steps and actions you can take.

PHASE ONE

Step One: *Make an honest assessment of the role Mammon plays in your life.*

We have to be honest with ourselves about what god we have chosen to follow or in what ways we are trying to serve two masters at the same time. I doubt there are many American Christians who do not have any struggles with *Mammon*—it is a great stronghold in our culture.

We may comfort ourselves about our lifestyles with passages from the Hebrew Bible about wealth as a blessing. We may hold onto Paul's words that it is the *love* of money that is the root of all evil and not money itself. We may even point to others—even other Christians—and justify ourselves by the fact that we are not rich compared to them. All these things can numb us to Jesus' teaching that *Mammon* can be a spiritual force in our hearts. It is not our heart condition that determines where we put our treasure, but rather where we have our treasure that will determine where our hearts are.

We have to come to grips with how we think money makes us feel, how it gives us value, and how it makes us think we are better than other people. We have to repent of the ways in which we trust it over God for our security, our futures, and our happiness. Until we honestly and seriously wrestle with the spiritual dimensions of *Mammon*, it will be hard for us to be generous and compassionate.

Actions:

* Do an analysis of what you spend your money on.

* If there are particular possessions, lifestyles, or investments to which you feel strongly attached, ask God to reveal to you if there are ways you trust in them more than him. Give ample time for this, maybe even a day-long prayer retreat.

* Ask friends who have chosen simpler lifestyles to look at your life and raise any concerns they have with your lifestyle choices.

Step Two: *Repent and experience the grace and generosity of God.*

When we acknowledge our own spiritual poverty, we can then return to the Father who runs out to us when he sees us still at a distance. Generosity and compassion do not spring from our natural state; they come from experiencing God. We can be merciful, compassionate, and generous because he is merciful, compassionate, and generous with us. We can love others because he has first loved us. If we do not understand God's grace, then we will be in danger of doing the right thing only to feel better about ourselves, which is really no different than how the Pharisees lived.

Spend time reflecting on God's grace in your salvation. Reflect on his amazing generosity toward you in the comfort you have enjoyed. Most of you reading this book have never suffered from hunger or homelessness or a lack of opportunities the way so many around the world have, so there is much we should be thankful for. Reflect on how he loves you as a child despite how you have rebelled against him. The more we are able to absorb his undeserved love, the more we will be able to love others in the same way.

Actions:

   * Make space to repent for the ways you may have trusted in *Mammon* over God.

   * Reflect on specific ways to repent, or change direction, in your life. Write them down if it helps.

   * Wait on God's mercy. Meditate on passages that deal with God's grace and compassion.

   * Ask him to make you more generous and compassionate.

Step Three: *Simplify your lifestyle in order to be more generous.*

How much stuff do you really need? How often do you need to eat out? How big a house do you have to have? What kind of car, if any, is necessary? Are we willing to use those things we have to love others—even if it means giving them up? There is no definitive line for what Christians can and cannot do, own and not own. We have to take these things before God, and the answer for each of us will be different. But we do need to take them before God; it is not good for us to live however we please and then assume God has "blessed" us.

Involving Christian community in this process is helpful. Most of us need to have others around us to help support the value for simplicity that is so often derided by our culture. Where our treasure is, there our hearts will be, and where our community of friends is, there our lifestyle will be. When some friends of ours who had always rented a home decided to buy a house, they brought people together to pray over the particular house they were interested in. They wanted to be sure that they were not being motivated by the world's values. They wanted to know that God's blessing was on their decision—we felt that it was. It is hard to maintain a commitment to simplicity in isolation.

Gary Vander Pol, Mako Nagasawa, and Rachel Anderson have developed a great group study, *Lazarus at the Gate*, which helps believers find their way through these issues of lifestyle and generosity together. The central idea is to form small communities of people into giving groups who try to simplify their lives and free up resources for the global poor. You can find their material online for free.

Actions:

* Decide to make one significant lifestyle change, or perhaps give up one possession that interferes with your ability to be obedient to God in this area.

* Reallocate some money or a possession, so that it benefits those who are economically challenged.

* Gather a group and work through *Lazarus at the Gate*.

Step Four: *Put yourself in a place where you can interact with people from a different class.*

Many of us are separated from the poor because of where we live. It is not the responsibility of people who are poor to come to us and make their needs visible; we have to cross the chasm that separates us. That may mean going to another part of town or another city or even another country. See for yourself what it is like for those who deal daily with violence, cockroaches, rats, hunger, hopelessness, and inadequate housing. Hear their stories about their struggles, joys, and the ways that God has met them in their lives. Go and see that the vast majority of the world does not live like middle-class Americans. In doing this, we will realize that our lifestyles are not sustainable for ourselves, let alone the rest of the planet. Stop reading books and articles about the poor and go out and actually meet real people. Pay special attention to those poor communities that tend to get overlooked; oftentimes, certain impoverished communities or assistance projects get a great deal of attention and investment while others are completely neglected.

In all of this, do not foolishly endanger yourself. We went out to a local restaurant with some friends who were visiting us a few years back. When we were leaving our lunch spot, our friend, who is a bit elderly, backed into another car in the parking lot. A young man came out and was extremely angry that his car had just been hit. I knew from the tattoos on his neck that he was a local gang member. I was able to calm him down and we settled the issue peacefully, but there was a stretch of time I was sure one of us was going to get hurt. When I mentioned to my friends afterward that this man was a gang member and that the situation could have ended very badly, the woman dismissed my concern. "Oh no," she said. "He seemed like a nice young man." If you are unfamiliar with the dangers of a new community, talk to people who can alert you to potential risks. You may choose to ignore those risks, but do not do so in ignorance.

Whatever it takes, get out of the gate, discover how your brothers and sisters are living, and in the midst of the ugliness of poverty, discover the beauty of the Savior's work among them.

Actions:

* Volunteer with a ministry that allows you to relate to the poor. Service ministries like soup kitchens and homeless shelters are fine, but seek out opportunities that encourage real interaction.

* Discover the disadvantaged areas around you and try to learn about who lives and ministers there. What are the issues they struggle with? Where have they experienced God?

* If a homeless person begs you for money, offer to buy them food and ask about their life.

* Do a short-term overseas missions trip that involves building relationships and learning from people versus just providing a service.

PHASE TWO

Step One: *Build relationships and learn compassion.*

People in the foreign land saw the suffering of the younger, prodigal son, but did not help him; the priest and the Levite saw a man dying on the side of the road and passed by on the other side; the rich man saw Lazarus, but did not come to his aid. These actions are contrasted with the father who sees his son at a distance, has compassion on him and runs to him, and the Good Samaritan who saw the man beaten by robbers and likewise had compassion on him and helped him. It is not enough to merely notice those in need; we have to learn to have compassion on them and act on their behalf. For us, this means that we need to build relationships with our poor brothers and sisters so that we can understand their struggles and love them.

You do not have to relocate to a poor neighborhood in order to do this, but you may have to do more than volunteer at a soup kitchen. Find a place where you can really learn about someone's life, but do not come in with an attitude of being a wealthy savior; meet the poor with a desire to learn from and with them. When you interact with people in a different class—higher or lower—you can start to understand them as real people and not just statistics. If the church you attend is not diverse socio-economically or if it is not committed to building cross-class relationships, consider finding one that is genuinely wrestling with these issues.

Some people may feel called to move into poorer communities. It is easier to see what the poor suffer when you walk with them, and it is also easier to see the weaknesses in a community that need to be addressed. However, relocation is no magic bullet; building deep relationships takes time and intention. I know many people who have chosen to live in poor communities but do not have deep relationships with the people around them. It requires constant work. If we want to have reciprocity in our relationships with the poor, we need to put ourselves into their world and let them into ours. To put a bit of a slant on what my Ghanaian pastor friend told me, you can't know every poor person in the world, but you can know some. Start with one person and see where the relationship leads you. For some people compassion comes easily; for others it requires walking in another person's shoes. If we are unwilling to learn compassion, we cannot then expect God or others to be compassionate toward us. In other words, we should offer to others the very thing we want offered to us.

Actions:

* Get to know one person or one family struggling in poverty and invest in their lives.

* Change churches or relocate to a poor community.

* Invite people from a different class into your home. Accept invitations to their homes and parties.

Step Two: *Learn to love and serve people in a way that empowers them and treats them as partners not projects.*

Previously, I mentioned that we work in a community on the outskirts of Johannesburg, South Africa. Like much of Africa, Johannesburg suffers not from too little generosity, but too much—or perhaps simply the wrong kinds of generosity. There are several dozen non-government organizations (NGOs) working in the community and probably hundreds of thousands of dollars being invested in various programs. And yet, when I sat with a number of local leaders, they said despite all the efforts and money poured into their community, very little had changed because no one had ever asked the community how *they* wanted to be helped. They cited the example of an NGO that offered parenting classes, and then complained when no one came. The NGO was convinced that residents needed to become better parents, but the residents did not share their perspective. Whenever leaders rose up in this community, an NGO or outside church would employ them to implement its own program, so there were very few indigenous initiatives. The projects that local leaders did develop were critiqued by outside experts without invitation. Everything these groups and churches did served only to discourage the local leaders, who in turn were afraid to say anything lest the money stop coming. To reverse this trend, we have been working to create a network of community leaders who have begun to set ground rules for how churches and NGOs partner with them in their community.

In many parts of the world, money pouring in from the

outside increases corruption and unhealthy competition between churches and agencies working for change. These agencies feel a need to tell the donor what they want to hear versus what will actually help them deal with poverty, and as a result very little ends up changing. One of our ministries in Los Angeles runs a tutoring program for student athletes at the local high school; however, unlike many other after school programs, this one depends on parental involvement. Parents are part of the planning and are asked to reflect on the program so that it achieves the goals they want to see happen. They reflect on what it will take for their kids to succeed in school and, therefore, what kind of program will achieve that end. As a result, there is a group of parents who are deeply invested in their children's education and success beyond the confines of the program.

It is important that we are generous with our time and money in a way that actually helps people, rather than disempowering them or making them dependent on outside resources. The underlying value must be to embrace our poor brothers and sisters as members of our family—members who are smart, resourceful, and have things to offer us as well. The best thing we can do is invest in them as people so that they can take responsibility for their lives and communities. Work gives us dignity; therefore, God's intention for his people is to become healthy, self-reliant, and interdependent, providing for themselves and their families as they are able, and giving generously with whatever resources they have (1 Tim 5:8, 2 Thess 3:6-13, Eph 4:28).

Actions:

* Reflect on whether your efforts to help the poor encourage them to take responsibility for their families and communities as they are able.

* Discover what assets those who are poor possess that can be built upon and supported.

* Encourage and participate in ministries that do not merely provide services, but invest in people so that they can become participants in their own transformation and the transformation of their community.

Step Three: *Work for systemic change.*

If we choose to become invested in the lives of our poorer brothers and sisters, we will quickly learn that there are whole systems that make it difficult for them to move out of poverty and into wholeness. It is natural to be compelled to change those systems, but there are a few dangers we can fall into in seeking to do so. First, it is often easy to work for larger change without any real relationship with the people you are trying to help. Thousands of people are shaping legislation and practices related to poverty without knowing any poor people. This is an obvious danger because the abstract poor are seen as statistics and stereotypes rather than complicated, unique individuals.

Second, real relationships and significant social change often take more time and effort than most of us have the patience for. Protesting and abstaining from certain commodities are easier than working for lasting change, though I am not saying there is no place for such action. We just have to ask if our efforts are actually helping someone or just making us feel better about ourselves.

One final danger is that those who work for larger change are often tempted to believe that they are good and that the opposition is evil and therefore deserves condemnation. However, this was not how Jesus responded to his enemies—and neither should we. I would also suggest that turning everyone into winners and losers does not promote real lasting change. More often than not, this kind of thinking disenfranchises those who lose so that they become enraged and potentially destructive in society. Permanent change is better achieved by winning people to our perspective, not by degrading them into submission.

Real change requires organization. Our elected officials are often assuaged by wealthy lobbyists and career concerns and may not have a poor community's best interest at heart. As such, we need to create or join organizations of people who can persevere in working on numerous issues of concern to the community, particularly of concern to the poor. Such groups can influence the political process and/or create new programs that better meet the needs of people.

Although we do need to remain loving, we cannot be afraid of conflict. Conflict is necessary for change and growth for us as individuals, for our churches, and for society as a whole. The Bible is full of people who confronted people in power in order to bring about justice and righteousness: Moses confronted Pharaoh, Samuel confronted Saul, Nathan confronted David, Tamar confronted Judah, Elijah confronted Ahab, and Nehemiah confronted the officials. Jesus did not avoid conflict with either his opponents or his followers. He spoke the truth to the Pharisees even when he knew it would cause them to plot against him. He accused Peter of acting like Satan by rejecting the teaching that the Son of Man had to die. If we have some idea that Christian love means not offending anyone, we can be sure that it did not come from Scripture or from Jesus. Speaking and living out the truth will bring conflict. When we do it well, the kingdom comes a little more fully.

The following suggestions for actions (except for the last one) all require a certain amount of expertise. As we cannot explore the technicalities here, I encourage you to seek out people in your community or region who know how to implement such efforts.

Actions:

  * Join a broad-based organizing network that represents both affluent institutions and poorer ones.

  * Target a particular issue that affects the poor (e.g. sex trafficking, immigrant's rights, or homelessness) and work with others over time to make a significant impact on policy and services offered.

  * Reflect with poorer people on what substantive transformation of their community would and should look like, and help them address these issues.

* Join a ministry that is committed to loving the poor, e.g. Servant Partners, InnerCHANGE, Servants to Asia's Urban Poor, Word Made Flesh, UNOH, or International Teams. Many other larger organizations also have branches that work with poor communities.

PHASE THREE: *REPEAT PHASES ONE AND TWO.*

It is often scary when God calls us to some new risk of faith, one in which we are made keenly aware of our need to trust Him. We grasp onto his hand like a frightened child, convinced that letting go would lead to certain death. However, after a while we find that our steps become easier and eventually do not seem risky at all. We may even cease to rely upon God to do the thing that at one time seemed impossible—we may start to believe we are doing it out of our own strength. We can reach a plateau in our journey with God and be tempted to settle down and build our house where it is comfortable.

In order to keep us from settling down spiritually, God often brings us back to where we have been in order to deepen the work he is doing in us. That first risk of faith is always the most life changing, but in time we discover that we have merely scratched the surface. The more we press forward with God, the more we realize we are dealing with the same issues at increasingly deeper levels. This process is no less true for how we use our wealth or treat our brothers and sisters. We will always battle *Mammon*'s grip on our lives and will continually fall short of loving the poor as Jesus loves them, but God will always be beckoning us to journey farther to some *other* rickety bridge so that we might confront our hearts of unbelief, know his grace and generosity more fully, and bear greater fruit in our lives. When we are paralyzed by fear at the thought of following after him, hopefully we will remember how he faithfully brought us over the previous chasm—and that each new crossing brings us closer to life.

Additionally, how we apply these teachings in one phase of our lives might be different than in other phases. Having children, taking care of older parents, and getting older ourselves will give us different contexts by which to understand God's will for our lives. Although the teaching remains the same, we are always changing and will continually wrestle with God to discover how he is calling us to respond anew.

Jesus has told us all we need to know; the only question for us is whether we will respond to what we have heard or scoff and continue to go on as we please. If we continue on in our present lifestyles, what else could possibly get our attention? If we ignore Moses and the prophets and even Jesus himself, what will get us to change before it is too late? Someone *has* risen from the dead and his Spirit continues to call out to us to follow him down the narrow road and away from the broad path that leads to destruction.

I am often reminded of C. S. Lewis' comment in his essay, "The Weight of Glory," that God finds our desires not too strong, but too weak.[4] We are too quick to settle for that which is worth so much less than what God promises us. We settle for cars and houses and lavish lifestyles when eternal treasures and friendships are offered us. Jesus calls us to be shrewd and invest in the eternal. He calls us to give up our trust in *Mammon* and set our eyes on that which does not perish. He calls us to have compassion on the outcast and the needy. He calls us to cross the chasm that separates us from our brothers and sisters caught in poverty so that we can be reunited as one family, one body with him as our head. He calls us to heed his (and Moses' and the prophets') warnings so that we cross the chasm soon, because a morning is coming for each of us when a bridge no longer spans it.

We have only to look at Jesus himself to find our model. He bridged the greatest chasm anyone ever has. He chose to leave his wealthy, comfortable home with the Father and went out to the gate to love those in need, laying down his life on their behalf. If we want to follow him, we have to get on that same bridge. Jesus does not send us to the other side of the chasm to minister to the poor and vulnerable, rather he pleads with us to join him there—with them—just like the father pleaded with his older son to join the party for his returned brother. If we want to be near Jesus, he is easy to find—he is at the celebration for our poor brothers and sisters on the other side of the chasm.

NOTES

Introduction

[1] United Nations, "The Millennium Development Goals Report 2012," 5. Cited 24 August 2014. Online: http://www.un.org/millenniumgoals/pdf/MDG%20Report%202012.pdf.

[2] United Nations, "Global Issues Vital Statistics 2010," n.p. [cited 24 August 2014]. Online: http://www.un.org/ en/ globalissues/briefingpapers/food/vitalstats.

[3] Bryant Myers, *Walking with the Poor: Principles and Practices in Transformational Development* (Maryknoll, NY: Orbis Books, 1999), 13.

[4] Jim Wallis, *The Call to Conversion: Recovering the Gospel for These Times* (New York: Harper and Row, 1981), 51.

[5] Ibid., 58.

Chapter 1

[1] I. Howard Marshall, *Commentary on Luke* (NIGCT; Grand Rapids: Eerdmans, 1978), 617.

[2] Joachim Jeremias, *Rediscovering the Parables* (New York: Charles Scribner's Sons, 1966), 105.

[3] Marshall, *Commentary on Luke*, 608.

[4] Viv Grigg, *Companion to the Poor* (Monrovia, CA: MARC, 1990), 39.

[5] Helmut Thielicke, *The Waiting Father: Sermons on the Parables of Jesus* (New York: Harper and Row, 1959), 26–7.

[6] Ibid., 32.

[7] Marshall, *Commentary on Luke*, 604.

[8] Thielicke, *The Waiting Father*, 38.

[9] Emerson O. Bradshaw, *Unconquerable Kagawa* (St. Paul: MacAlester Park, 1952), 84.

[10] Ibid., 85–90.

CHAPTER 2

[1] Marshall, *Commentary on Luke*, 617.

[2] Herman Hendrickx, *The Third Gospel for the Third World*, Vol. 3-B (Quezon City, Philippines: Claretian Publications, 2000), 171.

[3] Ibid.

[4] For theories on why some debtors are forgiven more than others see Hendrickx, *The Third Gospel for the Third World*, 173.

[5] For a broader discussion on the usury argument, see Marshall, *Commentary on Luke*, 614.

6 Walter E. Pilgrim, *Good News to the Poor* (Minneapolis: Augsburg, 1981), 126–7.

7 Hendrickx, *The Third Gospel for the Third World*, 174.

8 Ibid., 172.

9 William Barclay, *The Gospel of Luke* (Edinburgh: Saint Andrew, 1953), 215–6.

10 Hendrickx, *The Third Gospel for the Third World*, 184.

11 Jacques Ellul, *Money and Power* (Madison: InterVarsity, 1984), 75.

12 Ibid., 30–1.

13 John B. Hayes, *Sub-merge* (Ventura, CA: Regal, 2006), 71.

14 John Piper, *Desiring God* (Sisters, OR: Multnomah, 1986), 167.

15 Robert C. Linthicum, *Transforming Power: Biblical Strategies for Making a Difference in Your Community* (Downers Grove, IL: InterVarsity, 2003), 65.

CHAPTER 3

1 Ellul, *Money and Power*, 111.

2 J. M. Everts, "Financial Support," in *Dictionary of Paul and His Letters*, Edited by Gerald F. Hawthorne, Ralph P. Martin, and Daniel G. Reid (Downers Grove, IL: InterVarsity, 1993), 297.

[3] Richard J. Foster, *Celebration of Discipline: The Path to Spiritual Growth* (New York: HarperCollins, 1978), 190.

[4] John Piper, "Toward the Tithe and Beyond: How God Funds His Work" (Sermon). http://www.desiringgod.org/sermons/toward-the-tithe-and-beyond.

[5] Pilgrim, *Good News to the Poor*, 112.

[6] Ellul, *Money and Power*, 99.

[7] George Muller, *The Autobiography of George Muller* (New Kensington, PA: Whitaker, 1984), 195.

CHAPTER 4

[1] Ellul, *Money and Power*, 76.

[2] Barclay, *The Gospel of Luke*, 217.

[3] Marshall, *Commentary on Luke*, 624.

[4] Ellul, *Money and Power*, 75.

[5] Ibid.,

[6] Ibid., 80.

[7] Ibid., 75.

[8] Ibid., 93.

[9] Ibid., 94.

[10] For his argument that Babylon is symbolic for Rome in Revelation, see Darrell W. Johnson, *Discipleship on the Edge: An Expository Journey Through the Book of*

Revelation (Vancouver, BC: Regent College, 2004), 299.

[11] Ellul, *Money and Power*, 70.

[12] Ibid., 48.

[13] Ibid., 78.

[14] F.F. Bruce, *The Epistle to the Galatians* (NIGTC; Grand Rapids: Eerdmans, 1982), 27.

[15] Ibid., 147.

[16] Walter Brueggemann, "From Anxiety and Greed to Milk and Honey," *Sojourners* 38.2 (February 2009): 22. [cited 25 August 2014]. Online: http://sojo.net/magazine/2009/02/anxiety-and-greed-milk-and-honey.

[17] Ellul, *Money and Power*, 80.

[18] Wallis, *The Call to Conversion*, 60.

[19] Ellul, *Money and Power*, 97.

[20] Ibid., 110.

[21] Marshall, *Commentary on Luke*, 684.

[22] Ibid., 696.

CHAPTER 5

[1] Fred B. Craddock, *Luke* (IBC; Louisville: Westminster John Knox, 1990), 192.

[2] Barclay, *The Gospel of Luke*, 218.

[3] Jonathan Edwards, *Personal Narrative, The Works of*

Jonathan Edwards Vol. 1, (Carlisle, PA: Banner of Truth, 1974), xlvii-xlviii.

[4] Paul Tournier, *Guilt and Grace: A Psychological Study*, (New York: Harper & Row, 1962), 136.

[5] Robert C. Linthicum, *Building a People of Power: Equipping Churches to Transform Their Community*, (Waynesboro, GA: Authentic Media, 2005), 35.

CHAPTER 6

[1] Craddock, *Luke*, 193.

[2] N. T. Wright, *Simply Christian: Why Christianity Makes Sense* (New York: Harper and Row, 2006), 100.

[3] Alfred Edersheim, *The Life and Times of Jesus the Messiah*, (Peabody, MA: Hendrickson, 1993), 53.

[4] Wright, *Simply Christian*, 110.

[5] Marshall, *Commentary on Luke*, 184.

[6] Pilgrim, *Good News to the Poor*, 71.

[7] Barclay, *The Gospel of Luke*, 219.

[8] Marshall, *Commentary on Luke*, 630.

[9] Barclay, *The Gospel of Luke*, 220.

[10] Marshall, *Commentary on Luke*, 631–2.

[11] Gordon Fee, *The First Epistle to the Corinthians* (NICNT; Grand Rapids: Eerdmans, 1987), 295.

[12] Floyd V. Filson, *The Gospel According to St. Matthew* (New York: Harper & Row, 1960), 207.

[13] Donald G. Bloesch, *Freedom for Obedience: Evangelical Ethics in Contemporary Times* (San Francisco: Harper and Row, 1987), 71.

[14] Wright, *Simply Christian*, 219.

CHAPTER 7

[1] Marshall, *Commentary on Luke*, 635.

[2] Joseph A. Fitzmyer, *The Gospel According to Luke X–XXIV* (AB 28A; New York: Doubleday, 1985), 1130.

[3] Jeremias, *Rediscovering the Parables*, 145.

[4] Hendrickx, *The Third Gospel for the Third World*, 229.

[5] Ibid., 228.

[6] Ibid.

[7] Marshall, *Commentary on Luke*, 636.

[8] Hendrickx, *The Third Gospel for the Third World*, 231.

[9] Marshall argues that Hades is a reference to the state of human beings immediately after death as they await final judgment and should be contrasted with Gehenna, the final abode of the dead (Commentary on Luke, 636–7). However, Fitzmyer believes that this distinction between the two if far from certain and cites O. Bocher's argument that they are the same thing (*The Gospel According to Luke X–XXIV*, 855). Hendrickx agrees with Marshall but then goes

on to refer to the place where the rich man is as "hell" (*The Third Gospel for the Third World*, 233). It is probably wise not to infer too much about the specifics of the afterlife from this parable. What we know is that wherever the rich man is, it is a place of judgment and torment and there is no possibility of his condition being changed.

[10] Hendrickx, The *Third Gospel for the Third World*, 231.

[11] Ibid., 233.

[12] Marshall, *Commentary on Luke*, 637.

[13] Barclay, *The Gospel of Luke*, 222.

[14] Barna Group, "American Donor Trends," n.p. [cited 12 April 2013]. Online: https://www.barna.org/component/content/article/36-homepage-main-promo/606-barna-update-02-19-2013#.U_19LCiA_iI.

[15] Report of the 1978 Mission Consultation, 118th General Assembly of the Presbyterian Church in the United States, quoted by Kathleen and James McGinnis in *Parenting for Peace and Justice* (Maryknoll, NY: Orbis Books, 1981), 7.

CHAPTER 8

[1] Elizabeth Cohen and John Bonifield, "California's Dark Legacy of Forced Sterilizations," n.p. [cited 15 March 2012]. Online: http://www.cnn.com/2012/03/15/health/california-forced-sterilizations/.

[2] Kavitha A. Davidson, "Global Income Inequality: GlobalPost Puts America's Gap Between Rich and Poor in Perspective," n.p. [cited 22 January 2013]. Online: http://

www.huffingtonpost.com/2013/01/22/global-income-in-equality-globalpost_n_2526425.html.

3 Janet Napotilano, "Almost Half of Illegal Immigrants Entered U.S. Legally But Stayed After Visa Expired [cited 3 May 2011]. Online: http://www.hsgac.senate.gov/media/almost-half-of-illegal-immigrants-entered-us-legally-but-stayed-after-visa-expired.

4 Freetheslaves.net, "Slavery Still Exists: And It Could Be in Your Backyard," n.p. [cited 24 August 2014]. Online: https://www.freetheslaves.net/faq.

5 United Nations, "Global Issues Vital Statistics 2010," n.p. [cited 24 August 2014]. Online: http://www.un.org/en/globalissues/briefingpapers/food/vitalstats.

6 Anup Shah, "Poverty Facts and Stats," n.p. [cited 7 January 2013]. Online: http://www.globalissues.org/article/26/poverty-facts-and-stats.

7 Ibid

8 F. F. Bruce, *The Epistle to the Galatians* (NIGTC; Grand Rapids: Eerdmans, 1982), 126.

CHAPTER 9

1 R. C. H. Lenski, *The Interpretation of St. Paul's First and Second Epistles to the Corinthians* (Minneapolis: Augsburg, 1963), 1136.

2 Origen, *Contra Celsus, Book 3.* Quoted in Linthicum, *Building a People of Power*, 220.

3 Ibid.

4 Pilgrim, *Good News to the Poor*, 60.

CHAPTER 10

1 Myers, *Walking with the Poor*, 27.

2 Ibid., 73, 76.

3 Ibid., 74.

4 Linthicum, *Building a People of Power*, 118.

5 Ibid., 173.

CHAPTER 11

1 Jeremias, *Rediscovering the Parables*, 147.

2 Hendrickx, *The Third Gospel for the Third World*, 243.

3 Marshall, *Commentary on Luke*, 639.

4 Ibid.

5 Ibid.

6 Cornelius Houtman, *Exodus, Vol. 3* (Leuven, Belguim: Peeters, 2000), 218–9.

7 Ibid., 218.

8 Ibid.

9 Gerhard Von Rad, *Deuteronomy* (OTL; Philadelphia: Westminster John Knox, 1966), 26.

[10] Walter Brueggemann, *Deuteronomy* (AOTC; Nashville: Abingdon, 2001), 166.

[11] Ibid.

[12] J. A. Thompson, *Deuteronomy* (TOTC; Downers Grove, IL: InterVarsity, 2008), 188.

[13] Pilgrim, *Good News to the Poor,* 23.

[14] Ibid., 24.

[15] Richard N. Boyce, *Leviticus and Numbers* (WC; Louisville: Westminster John Knox, 2008), 102.

[16] Pilgrim, *Good News to the Poor,* 24.

CHAPTER 12

[1] Paul D. Hanson, *Isaiah 40-66* (IBC; Louisville: Westminster John Knox, 1995), 188.

[2] Francis L. Andersen and David Noel Freedman, *Amos* (AB 24A; New York: Doubleday, 1989), 308.

[3] Roy L. Honeycutt, *Amos and His Message: An Expository Commentary* (Nashville: Broadman, 1963), 37.

[4] Andersen and Freedman, *Amos*, 313.

[5] Honeycutt, *Amos and His Message*, 39.

[6] Ibid.

[7] Christopher J. H. Wright, *The Message of Ezekiel: A New Heart and a New Spirit* (Downers Grove, IL: InterVarsity, 2001), 20, 41.

[8] For a full treatment of this section of Ezekiel, see Linthicum, *Transforming Power*, 41–56.

[9] Nancy R. Bowen, *Ezekiel* (AOTC; Nashville: Abingdon Press, 2010), 137.

[10] Ibid., 69.

[11] Ibid., 137.

[12] Linthicum, *Building a People of Power*, 10.

[13] Hanson, *Isaiah 40–66*, 185.

[14] Ibid., 186.

[15] Jan L. Koole, *Isaiah III, Vol. 3* (Leuven, Belguim: Peeters, 2001), 116.

[16] Hanson, *Isaiah 40–66*, 207.

[17] Jacob M. Myers, *Ezra and Nehemiah* (AB 14; New York: Doubleday, 1965), 96.

[18] Ibid., 130.

CHAPTER 13

[1] The argument that Josiah discovered a version of Deuteronomy is based upon the observation that the reforms he enacted reflect an understanding of Deuteronomy specifically. See Von Rad, Deuteronomy pg. 27.

[2] David J. Bosch, *A Spirituality of the Road* (Eugene: Wipf and Stock, 2000), 13.

[3] Ibid., 15.

Notes

[4] C.S. Lewis, *The Weight of Glory and Other Addresses* (Grand Rapids: Eerdmans, 1965), 2.

ACKNOWLEDGEMENTS

THE TOPICS OF WEALTH, POVERTY, THE RICH, AND THE POOR are dauntingly complex. I have learned a great deal from those who have been addressing these issues for decades and have been willing to pass on some of their understanding to me either personally or in books. I am grateful for the mentorship and instruction of Robert Linthicum as well as Viv Grigg. John Perkins, who was living in a poor community near my college when I was a student, challenged me to relocate and learn to reconcile with people different from myself. I ran into Jim Wallis at a conference this past year and was able to thank him for his book The Call to Conversion, which was so important to my early wrestling with these topics. Jacques Ellul forever changed my view of wealth with his book Money and Power. I am not planning on running into him soon, and so my personal thanks will have to wait.

In this book, I deal significantly with the idea of grace and how it directs us away from self-justification but toward obedience. There is no one to whom I am more indebted for my understanding of this than Daniel Fuller. He caused me to dig deeply into Paul's letter to the Galatians which has become the central scripture of my life. Though the letter has little to do directly with the main subject of this book, its theology, and Dan's teaching, could not help but seep into my writing.

As I have struggled with the best way to deal with systemic change and the empowerment of the poor, I have appreciated the mentorship of several community organizers including Sr. Judy Donovan, Ken Fujimoto, and Rebecca Gifford.

My parents, Dick and Brenda, were the first to model generosity and simplicity to me. Though living on a pastor's salary meant that our lifestyle was different than most of our friends, my childhood was in no way marred because they chose not to buy me the genuine Members Only jacket or OP corduroy shorts (I realize I am dating myself). They were sacrificially generous with their time and the resources they had. My childhood made me realize that happiness does not consist in the excess of things or in storing up wealth for some future enjoyment. Even now in retirement, my parents continue to give all they can to their children and grandchildren.

I am grateful for all of the people I have worked with over the past sixteen years I have been with Servant Partners. I am sure I have learned more from them than I am even completely aware. My thanks to those whose ministry and personal stories I have used in the book; Trevor Davies, Jean Luc Krieg, Chris Rattay, Sara Stephens, Chris and Maureen Hodge, and Tom and Bree Hsieh. I am particularly thankful for those Servant Partners staff who have studied Luke 15 and 16 with me every year for the past ten years as part of their orientation. Though I was supposed to be their teacher, every class gave me some new insight into the text that forms the framework for this book. For the past number of years, we have studied it together in the sweltering heat of South East Asia, bombarded by the distractions that only a squatter community can provide. These conditions were never ideal for academic focus, but it has seemed appropriate to live among the poor while we wrestle with what Jesus says about them. The idea for this book came from one of those studies.

I am deeply indebted to my wife, Lisa, who has been my partner on this journey. She has been my greatest model of love and compassion. Together, we have struggled to discern God's will for our lives, sought to care for our poor neighbors, and labored to build an organization working for transformation.

Of course, no one deserves more thanks for this book than those people either born into poverty or still living in it who have shared their stories and lives with me; Ray and Annie, Ema Smith, Cora Giamzon, Ingrid King, Reyna and Lorenzo Torres, Anathi Pefile, Orapeleng "Ora" Letsholo, Yut, Dadchaneeporn "Kaew" Ariso, and Aling Nena. There are several other people's stories I tell but I have changed their names to respect their privacy.

I was struck by the humility of N.T. Wright who wrote in the preface to his book The New Testament and the People of God that he is quite certain that a "good proportion" of what he says is wrong or at least flawed, though he does not realize it. I feel a need to make the same admission. Though I state things confidently at times, I know that my understanding is flawed because I am flawed, and I pray that God and my readers will extend mercy to me.

I do also address social, political, and economic topics in the book and I am aware that not all of my readers will agree with my perspectives. Even if we agree completely on the interpretation of scripture (which is, itself, unlikely), we will find some differences in our application to the modern world. I am not bothered by this as long as we all genuinely wrestle with what Jesus is saying to us. After all, my opinion is of little worth. My readers must take these things to God and trust that he will speak.